Betty Crocker's
Timesaving
Cookbook

Betty Crocker's Timesaving Cookbook

Random House, Inc. New York

Originally published as BETTY CROCKER'S WORKING WOMAN'S COOKBOOK

FOREWORD

No matter how many other responsibilities you have, you are always aware of a basic concern — the management of your own kitchen. Even with willing help from other family members in marketing, cooking, table-setting and cleanup, it is you and you alone who are in charge.

In-home food service, the production of nearly 1000 meals a year — breakfasts, lunches, lunches-to-go and dinners, plus snacks — for every member of the household, adds up to really big business. So it makes sense to apply some timesaving skills to your kitchen activities.

Betty Crocker's Timesaving Cookbook is designed to do just this — help you manage valuable time and energy in preparing nutritious, home-cooked meals for you and your family. It begins with more than 280 practical, appealing recipes for main dishes, vegetables, salads, breads, appetizers, desserts and beverages — even for dry mixes that you can make yourself for spur-of-the-moment biscuits, muffins and cookies. And, of course, they all were developed and thoroughly tested for your satisfaction in the Betty Crocker Kitchens.

Some are quick and easy recipes to prepare and serve right now at the close of a hectic day. Others are "do-aheads" (each flagged with a red spoon symbol ) for a few free hours, whenever they may be. The "do-aheads" stored in the refrigerator or freezer are like money in the bank — good investments that pay high dividends for family meals or entertaining on days when you literally have no time to cook. And each recipe is complete with recommended storage time, and heating and serving directions.

Finally, we've filled a special chapter (page 148) with specific tips on organizing your kitchen workspace, planning the work flow, and using shortcuts and special appliances to streamline food preparation. You'll find microwave directions to save time, and pressure cooker instructions for quick cooking of less-tender economy cuts of meat. Check out our menu suggestions and food purchasing plans and learn to use your refrigerator and freezer for maximum efficiency. All this and more will help you achieve a smooth running operation and show a handsome reward in delicious meals you and your family will enjoy.

Betty Crocker

Copyright © 1982 by General Mills, Inc., Minneapolis, Minnesota

All rights reserved under International and Pan-American Copyright Conventions. Published in the United States by Random House, Inc., New York, and simultaneously in Canada by Random House of Canada Limited, Toronto.

Library of Congress Cataloging in Publication Data   Crocker, Betty. Rev. ed. of: Betty Crocker's Working Woman's Cookbook, c1982.

Includes index. 1. Cookery. I. Crocker, Betty. Working Woman's Cookbook. II. Title. III. Title: Timesaving Cookbook.
TX652.C832   1985   641.5'55   84-26255   ISBN 0-394-54539-7

Manufactured in the United States of America   468975

Contents

Meat Main Dishes

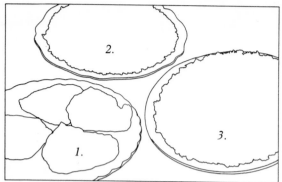

1. Pork Chops with Kiwi Sauce, 2. Lamb Veronique,
3. Steak with Mushroom-Wine sauce.

Steak with Mushroom-Wine Sauce

6 to 8 servings

1½ - pound beef boneless bottom or top round,
       tip or chuck steak (¾ to 1 inch thick)
1   envelope (about 1¹/₁₆ ounces) instant meat
       marinade
     Salt and pepper
1   package (6 ounces) stuffing mix
1   envelope (about ¾ ounce) brown gravy mix
¾   cup cold water
¼   cup dry red wine
1   can (4 ounces) mushroom stems and pieces,
       drained

Diagonally slash outer edge of fat at 1-inch intervals to prevent curling (do not cut into lean). Marinate beef as directed on envelope of meat marinade. Set oven control to broil and/or 550°. Place beef on rack in broiler pan. Broil with top 2 to 3 inches from heat until brown, about 10 minutes. Sprinkle with salt and pepper; turn. Broil until brown and desired doneness, about 12 minutes for medium.

Prepare stuffing mix as directed on package. Mix gravy mix, water and wine in 1-quart saucepan. Heat to boiling over medium heat, stirring constantly. Stir in mushrooms. Heat until mushrooms are hot, about 2 minutes. Cut beef into thin slices; arrange on stuffing. Serve with mushroom-wine sauce.

Onion-Topped Steak

6 servings

1½ - pound beef boneless bottom or top round,
       tip or chuck steak (about ½ inch thick)
1   envelope (about 1¹/₁₆ ounces) instant meat
       marinade
2   tablespoons sugar
1   tablespoon cornstarch
½   teaspoon dry mustard
¼   teaspoon salt
1   cup water
1   teaspoon finely shredded orange peel
½   cup orange juice
1   tablespoon lemon juice
1   can (3 ounces) French fried onions

Diagonally slash outer edge of fat at 1-inch intervals to prevent curling (do not cut into lean). Marinate beef as directed on envelope of meat marinade. Mix sugar, cornstarch, mustard and salt in 1½-quart saucepan. Stir in water, orange peel, orange juice and lemon juice. Cook, stirring constantly, until mixture thickens and boils. Boil and stir 1 minute.

Set oven control to broil and/or 550°. Place beef on rack in broiler pan. Broil with top 2 to 3 inches from heat until brown, about 8 minutes. Brush with orange sauce; turn. Broil until desired doneness, 8 to 10 minutes for medium. Brush with orange sauce; sprinkle with onions. Serve with sauce.

BROILING BEEF STEAKS

Slash outer edge of fat at 1-inch intervals to prevent curling. Place steaks on rack in broiler pan. Set oven control to broil and/or 550°. Broil until steaks are brown; sprinkle with salt and pepper if desired. Turn steak; broil until brown and desired doneness.

Total Cooking Time in Minutes			
Thickness	Inches from Heat	Rare (140°F)	Medium (160°F)
1 inch	2 to 3	15 to 20	20 to 25
1½ inches	3 to 5	25 to 30	30 to 35

Steak with Horseradish

6 servings

1½ - *pound beef boneless bottom or top round,*
    tip or chuck steak (³/₄ to 1 inch thick)
1   *envelope (about 1¹/₁₆ ounces) instant meat*
    marinade
    Salt and pepper
    Horseradish Sauce (below)

Diagonally slash outer edge of fat at 1-inch intervals to prevent curling (do not cut into lean). Marinate beef as directed on envelope of meat marinade.

Set oven control to broil and/or 550°. Place beef on rack in broiler pan. Broil with top 2 to 3 inches from heat until brown, about 10 minutes. Sprinkle with salt and pepper; turn. Broil until brown and desired doneness, about 12 minutes for medium. Prepare Horseradish Sauce; serve with beef.

Horseradish Sauce

Beat ½ cup whipping cream in chilled 1-quart bowl until stiff. Fold in 3 tablespoons well-drained prepared horseradish and ½ teaspoon salt.

Beef Steaks and Carrots

4 servings

¹/₃ *cup all-purpose flour*
½ *teaspoon salt*
¹/₈ *teaspoon pepper*
4 *beef cubed steaks (about 4 ounces each)*
2 *tablespoons vegetable oil*
1 *jar (16 ounces) whole baby carrots, drained,*
1 *can (10½ ounces) condensed onion soup*
½ *teaspoon parsley flakes*
¹/₈ *teaspoon dried rosemary leaves, crushed*

Mix flour, salt and pepper; coat beef with flour mixture. Heat oil over medium-high heat until hot. Cook beef in oil until brown, about 4 minutes on each side. (Add more oil if necessary.) Stir in remaining ingredients. Heat to boiling; reduce heat. Simmer uncovered until carrots are hot, about 5 minutes.

Sweet-and-Sour Stir-Fried Beef

Sweet-and-Sour Stir-Fried Beef

5 servings

1 *pound beef flank steak*
1 *tablespoon cornstarch*
1 *tablespoon cold water*
3 *tablespoons vegetable oil*
1 *medium onion, cut into 1-inch pieces*
1 *can (8¹/₄ ounces) pineapple chunks, drained*
½ *cup water*
¹/₄ *cup sugar*
¹/₄ *cup white vinegar*
1 *tablespoon instant chicken bouillon*
1 *tablespoon soy sauce*
1 *medium green pepper, cut into 1-inch pieces*
2 *medium tomatoes, each cut into eighths*

Trim excess fat from beef; cut beef with grain into 2-inch strips. Cut strips across grain into ¹/₈-inch slices. Mix cornstarch and 1 tablespoon water. Heat oil in 12-inch skillet or wok over medium-high heat until hot. Add beef and onion; cook and stir until beef is brown, about 3 minutes. Stir in pineapple, ½ cup water, the sugar, vinegar, instant bouillon and soy sauce. Heat to boiling. Stir in cornstarch mixture. Cook and stir 1 minute. Stir in green pepper and tomatoes; cook and stir 1 minute. Serve with hot cooked rice if desired.

Flemish Beef Roast with Vegetables

Flemish Beef Roast with Vegetables

8 servings

6   slices bacon, cut into ¹/₂-inch pieces
4 - pound beef arm, blade or cross rib roast
¹/₄ cup packed brown sugar
2   teaspoons salt
¹/₂ teaspoon garlic powder
¹/₂ teaspoon pepper
¹/₂ teaspoon dried thyme leaves
³/₄ cup water
¹/₂ cup beer

Have ready at serving time:

1   package (20 ounces) frozen vegetables for stew
¹/₂ cup cold water
¹/₄ cup all-purpose flour

Fry bacon in 4-quart Dutch oven until crisp. Remove bacon with slotted spoon; drain on paper towels. Drain fat, reserving 2 tablespoons in pan. Cook beef in fat over medium heat, turning occasionally, until brown; drain. Add brown sugar, salt, garlic powder, pepper, thyme, bacon, water and beer. Heat to boiling; reduce heat. Cover and simmer just until beef is tender, 2½ to 3 hours. (To serve immediately, continue as directed in TO SERVE.) Cover and refrigerate beef and broth separately. Store no longer than 48 hours.

TO SERVE: About 45 minutes before serving, remove fat from broth. Heat beef and broth to boiling. Add vegetables; cover and simmer until beef is hot and vegetables are tender, about 20 minutes. Remove beef and vegetables to warm platter. Drain broth, reserving 2 cups in pan. Shake water and flour in covered container; stir into broth. Heat to boiling, stirring constantly. Boil and stir 1 minute. Serve with beef and vegetables.

Pressure Cooker Directions: Fry bacon in 6-quart pressure cooker until crisp. Remove bacon with slotted spoon; drain on paper towels. Drain fat, reserving 2 tablespoons in pan. Cook beef in fat over medium heat, turning occasionally, until brown; drain. Add brown sugar, salt, garlic powder, pepper, thyme, bacon, water and beer. Following manufacturer's directions, cover and cook at 15 pounds pressure 35 to 45 minutes. Cool 5 minutes; reduce pressure. Add vegetables. Heat to boiling; reduce heat. Simmer uncovered, stirring occasionally, until vegetables are tender, about 10 minutes. Remove beef and vegetables to warm platter; keep warm. Continue as directed in TO SERVE.

Fruited Pot Roast

10 servings

3 - pound beef boneless chuck roast
2 tablespoons vegetable oil
1 cup dry red wine
1 large onion, sliced
2 teaspoons salt
1/2 teaspoon pepper

Have ready at serving time:

2 medium carrots, cut into 1/4-inch slices
1 package (8 ounces) mixed dried fruit
1 medium green pepper, cut into 1-inch pieces

Cook beef in oil in 4-quart Dutch oven, turning occasionally, until brown; drain. Add wine, onion, salt and pepper. Heat to boiling; reduce heat. Cover and simmer, turning occasionally, until beef is tender, about 2½ hours. (To serve immediately, continue as directed in TO SERVE.) Cover and refrigerate beef and broth separately. Store no longer than 48 hours.

TO SERVE: About 45 minutes before serving, remove fat from broth. Heat beef, broth, carrots and fruit to boiling; reduce heat. Cover and simmer, stirring occasionally, until carrots are almost tender, about 25 minutes. Add green pepper. Heat to boiling; reduce heat. Simmer uncovered until green pepper is crisp-tender, about 5 minutes. Remove beef and vegetables to warm platter. Skim fat from broth. Serve broth with beef.

■ *Pressure Cooker Directions:* Cook beef in oil in 6-quart pressure cooker, until brown; drain. Add wine, onion, salt and pepper. Following manufacturer's directions, cover and cook at 15 pounds pressure 35 to 45 minutes. Cool 5 minutes; reduce pressure. Add carrots and fruit. Cover and cook at 15 pounds pressure 2 minutes. Cool 5 minutes; reduce pressure. Continue as directed in TO SERVE.

Spanish Rice and Beef

6 servings

2½ cups cut-up cooked beef
1 medium onion, chopped (about 1/2 cup)
2 tablespoons margarine or butter
2 cups water
1 cup uncooked regular rice
1 can (16 ounces) stewed tomatoes
1 teaspoon chili powder
3/4 teaspoon salt
1/2 teaspoon dried oregano leaves
1/8 teaspoon pepper

Cook and stir beef and onion in margarine in 10-inch skillet until onion is tender. Stir in remaining ingredients. Heat to boiling; reduce heat. Cover and simmer until rice is tender, about 30 minutes. (A small amount water can be added if necessary.)

SPANISH RICE AND GROUND BEEF: Substitute 1 pound ground beef for the cooked beef. Omit margarine. Cook and stir ground beef and onion in 10-inch skillet until beef is light brown; drain. Continue as directed.

Pepper-Beef Sauce

6 servings

1 medium onion, chopped (about 1/2 cup)
2 tablespoons olive oil or vegetable oil
2 cups cut-up cooked beef
2 medium green peppers, coarsely chopped
2 cans (15 ounces each) tomato sauce special
1/2 teaspoon dried basil leaves
1/2 teaspoon dried oregano leaves
1/4 teaspoon garlic salt
1 package (7 ounces) spaghetti
1/2 cup grated Parmesan cheese

Cook and stir onion in oil in 10-inch skillet until tender. Stir in beef, green peppers, tomato sauce, basil, oregano and garlic salt. Heat to boiling; reduce heat. Cover and simmer 15 minutes. Cook spaghetti as directed on package; drain. Serve sauce over spaghetti; sprinkle with cheese.

Mexican-Style Beef

6 to 8 servings

2 - pound beef bottom round roast
1   small onion, cut into fourths
1   tablespoon chili powder
2   teaspoons salt
½   teaspoon pepper
2   cloves garlic, crushed

Have ready at serving time:

1   medium onion, chopped
2   tablespoons vegetable oil
1   can (16 ounces) stewed tomatoes
½   cup sliced pimiento-stuffed olives
½   cup raisins
½   teaspoon ground cinnamon
3   cups hot cooked rice

Place beef, onion, chili powder, salt, pepper and garlic in 4-quart Dutch oven. Add enough water to cover. Heat to boiling; reduce heat. Cover and simmer until beef is tender, 2 to 2½ hours; drain. Cool beef slightly; shred into pieces with 2 forks. (To serve immediately, continue as directed in TO SERVE.) Cover and refrigerate no longer than 48 hours.

TO SERVE: About 30 minutes before serving, cook and stir onion in oil in 10-inch skillet over medium heat until tender. Stir in beef, tomatoes, olives, raisins and cinnamon. Heat to boiling; reduce heat. Cover and simmer, stirring occasionally, 15 minutes. Uncover and simmer 5 minutes longer. Serve over rice. Sprinkle with slivered almonds if desired.

■ *Pressure Cooker Directions:* Place beef, onion, chili powder, salt, pepper, garlic and 1 cup water in 4-quart pressure cooker. Following manufacturer's directions, cover and cook at 15 pounds pressure 35 to 45 minutes. Cool 5 minutes. Reduce pressure; drain. Cool beef slightly; shred into small pieces with 2 forks. Continue as directed in TO SERVE.

Mexican-Style Beef

Enchiladas

2 meals - 6 servings each

Mexican-Style Beef (page 12)
2   cans (15 ounces each) tomato sauce
1   cup water
2   tablespoons chili powder
1   teaspoon dried oregano leaves
1/2 teaspoon ground cumin
24 flour or corn tortillas (6 inches in diameter)
3   cups shredded Cheddar or Monterey Jack
      cheese (about 12 ounces)

Prepare Mexican-Style Beef except — omit rice. Heat tomato sauce, water, chili powder, oregano and cumin to boiling; reduce heat. Simmer uncovered, stirring occasionally, 10 minutes. Pour about half of the sauce into ungreased 9 × 1¼-inch pie plate.

Prepare tortillas as directed on package. Dip 1 tortilla into tomato sauce to coat both sides. Spoon about 1 heaping tablespoon beef mixture down center of tortilla. Sprinkle with 2 teaspoons cheese. Roll tortilla around filling. Repeat with remaining tortillas. Place tortillas, seam sides down, in 2 ungreased 13 × 9 × 2-inch baking pans. Pour half of the remaining sauce over each pan of enchiladas. Sprinkle each pan with half of the remaining cheese. (To serve 1 pan immediately, cook uncovered in 350° oven until hot and bubbly, about 20 minutes.) Cover and refrigerate no longer than 24 hours.

TO SERVE: About 35 minutes before serving, heat 1 pan Enchiladas uncovered in 350° oven until hot and bubbly, about 30 minutes. Serve with sour cream if desired.

GROUND BEEF ENCHILADAS: Cook and stir 2 pounds ground beef, 1 large onion, chopped (about 1 cup), and 2 cloves garlic, finely chopped, until beef is light brown; drain. Stir in 2 teaspoons salt and 1 bottle (8 ounces) taco sauce. Substitute ground beef mixture for the Mexican-Style Beef.

New England Boiled Dinner

6 to 8 servings

2½ - to 3-pound beef corned brisket or round

Have ready at serving time:

6   small carrots
6   small onions
3   medium potatoes, cut into halves
1   small head cabbage, cut into 6 wedges

Pour just enough cold water on beef in 4-quart Dutch oven to cover. Heat to boiling; reduce heat. Cover and simmer until beef is tender, about 2 hours. (To serve immediately, continue as directed in TO SERVE.) Cover and refrigerate beef and 5 cups of the broth separately. Store no longer than 48 hours.

TO SERVE: About 35 minutes before serving, remove fat from broth. Heat beef, broth, carrots, onions and potatoes to boiling; reduce heat. Cover and simmer until beef is hot and vegetables are tender, about 20 minutes. Remove beef and vegetables to warm platter; keep warm. Add cabbage to broth. Heat to boiling; reduce heat. Simmer uncovered until crisp-tender, about 15 minutes. Serve cabbage with beef and vegetables.

■ *Pressure Cooker Directions:* Place beef and 4 cups cold water in 6-quart pressure cooker. Following manufacturer's directions, cover and cook at 15 pounds pressure 45 minutes. Cool 5 minutes; reduce pressure. Add carrots, onions and potatoes. Cover and cook at 15 pounds pressure 5 minutes. Cool 5 minutes; reduce pressure. Remove beef and vegetables to warm platter; keep warm. Add cabbage to broth. Heat to boiling; reduce heat. Simmer uncovered until crisp-tender, about 15 minutes. Serve cabbage with beef and vegetables.

Swiss Steak

6 servings

3 tablespoons all-purpose flour
1 teaspoon dry mustard
½ teaspoon salt
1½ - pound beef boneless bottom or top round,
     tip or chuck steak (½ inch thick)
2 tablespoons vegetable oil
1 can (16 ounces) whole tomatoes
2 cloves garlic, finely chopped

Have ready at serving time:

1 cup water
1 large onion, sliced
1 large green pepper, sliced

Mix flour, mustard and salt. Sprinkle 1 side of beef with half of the flour mixture; pound in. Turn beef and pound in remaining flour mixture. Cut beef into 6 pieces. Heat oil in 10-inch skillet until hot. Cook beef over medium heat until brown, about 15 minutes. Add tomatoes (with liquid) and garlic; break up tomatoes with fork. Heat to boiling; reduce heat. Cover and simmer until beef is tender, about 1 hour. (To serve immediately, add water, onion and green pepper. Heat to boiling; reduce heat. Cover and simmer until vegetables are tender, 5 to 8 minutes.) Cover and refrigerate no longer than 48 hours.

TO SERVE: About 15 minutes before serving, add water, onion and green pepper to Swiss Steak. Heat to boiling; reduce heat. Cover and simmer until beef is hot and vegetables are tender, 5 to 8 minutes.

■ *Pressure Cooker Directions:* Prepare and cook beef in hot oil in 4-quart pressure cooker as directed above. Add tomatoes (with liquid) and garlic; break up tomatoes with fork. Following manufacturer's directions, cover and cook at 15 pounds pressure 25 minutes. Cool 5 minutes; reduce pressure. Omit water. Add onion and green pepper. Heat to boiling; reduce heat. Simmer uncovered until beef is hot and vegetables are tender, 5 to 8 minutes.

Beef Stew

6 servings

1½ pounds beef for stew, cut into ½-inch pieces
1 tablespoon shortening
1½ cups water
1 can (10½ ounces) condensed beef broth
⅛ teaspoon pepper

Have ready at serving time:

2 large potatoes, cut into 1½-inch pieces
3 medium carrots, cut into 1-inch pieces
2 medium stalks celery, cut into 1-inch pieces
1 medium onion, cut into 1-inch pieces
1 teaspoon salt
1 bay leaf
½ cup cold water
2 tablespoons all-purpose flour

Cook and stir beef in shortening in 4-quart Dutch oven until brown, about 15 minutes. Add 1½ cups water, the broth and pepper. Heat to boiling; reduce heat. Cover and simmer until beef is tender, 2 to 2½ hours. (To serve immediately, continue as directed in TO SERVE.) Cover and refrigerate no longer than 48 hours.

TO SERVE: About 50 minutes before serving, remove fat from broth. Add potatoes, carrots, celery, onion, salt and bay leaf. Heat to boiling; reduce heat. Cover and simmer until vegetables are tender, about 30 minutes. Shake ½ cup water and the flour in tightly covered container; gradually stir into beef mixture. Heat to boiling, stirring constantly. Boil and stir 1 minute.

■ *Pressure Cooker Directions:* Cook and stir beef in shortening in 4-quart pressure cooker. Add ¼ cup water, the broth and pepper. Following manufacturer's directions, cover and cook at 15 pounds pressure 12 minutes. Cool 5 minutes; reduce pressure. Add potatoes, carrots, celery, onion, salt and bay leaf. Cover and cook at 15 pounds pressure 3 minutes. Cool 5 minutes; reduce pressure. Shake ½ cup water and the flour in tightly covered container; gradually stir into beef mixture. Heat to boiling, stirring constantly. Boil and stir 1 minute.

Savory Beef Short Ribs

8 servings

4   pounds beef short ribs, cut into pieces
2   tablespoons vegetable oil
1   can (10½ ounces) condensed beef broth
1   jar (5 ounces) prepared horseradish
½   teaspoon salt

Have ready at serving time:

2   large onions, sliced
¼   cup cold water
2   tablespoons all-purpose flour
½   cup dairy sour cream

Cook beef in oil in 4-quart Dutch oven over medium heat until brown; drain. Stir in broth, horseradish and salt. Heat to boiling; reduce heat. Cover and simmer until beef is tender, about 2 hours. (To serve immediately, remove beef from broth; keep warm. Add onions. Cover and simmer until onions are tender, 5 to 8 minutes. Skim excess fat from broth. Add enough water to broth to measure 2 cups. Shake water and flour in tightly covered container; gradually stir into broth. Heat to boiling, stirring constantly. Boil and stir 1 minute; remove from heat. Stir in sour cream. Pour over beef.) Cover and refrigerate no longer than 48 hours.

TO SERVE: About 30 minutes before serving, remove fat from Savory Beef Short Ribs. Add onions. Heat to boiling; reduce heat. Simmer uncovered until beef is hot, about 20 minutes. Remove beef to warm platter; keep warm. Add enough water to broth to measure 2 cups. Shake water and flour in tightly covered container; gradually stir into broth. Heat to boiling, stirring constantly. Boil and stir 1 minute; remove from heat. Stir in sour cream; pour over beef.

■ *Pressure Cooker Directions:* Cook beef in oil in 6-quart pressure cooker over medium heat until brown; drain. Stir in broth, horseradish and salt. Following manufacturer's directions, cover and cook at 15 pounds pressure 25 minutes. Cool 5 minutes; reduce pressure. Add onions. Heat to boiling; reduce heat. Simmer uncovered until onions are tender, 5 to 8 minutes. Remove beef to warm platter; keep warm. Skim excess fat from broth. Drain broth, reserving 2 cups in pan. Shake water and flour in tightly covered container; gradually stir into broth. Heat to boiling, stirring constantly. Boil and stir 1 minute; remove from heat. Stir in sour cream; pour over beef.

Beef-Mushroom Mix

3 meals - 4 or 5 servings each

6	medium onions, sliced
1½	pounds mushrooms, sliced, or 2 cans (8 ounces each) mushroom stems and pieces, drained
3	cloves garlic, finely chopped
⅓	cup margarine or butter
2	to 4 tablespoons vegetable oil
½	cup all-purpose flour
2	teaspoons salt
2	teaspoons paprika
4½	pounds beef for stew, cut into 1-inch pieces
2	cans (10½ ounces each) condensed beef broth
1	cup water
½	teaspoon dried marjoram leaves
½	teaspoon dried thyme leaves

Cook and stir onions, mushrooms and garlic in margarine in 4-quart Dutch oven over medium heat until onions are tender. Remove vegetables with slotted spoon and reserve. Add oil to Dutch oven. Mix flour, salt and paprika; coat beef with flour mixture. Cook and stir about ⅓ of the beef in oil until brown; repeat with remaining beef, adding 1 to 2 tablespoons oil if necessary. Mix beef, broth, water, marjoram and thyme in Dutch oven. Heat to boiling; reduce heat. Cover and simmer until beef is tender, 1½ to 2 hours. Stir in reserved vegetables. Refrigerate until cool. Divide beef mixture (about 4 cups each) among three 1-quart freezer containers. Cover, label and freeze no longer than 3 months. Use for Beef Burgundy (right), Curried Beef (right) or Beef Stroganoff (page 17).

Beef Burgundy

4 servings

1	container Beef-Mushroom Mix (left)
¼	cup water
1	cup dry red wine
	Snipped parsley

Dip container of Beef-Mushroom Mix into very hot water just to loosen. Place frozen block in 3-quart saucepan. Add water. Heat uncovered over medium heat, stirring occasionally, until hot, about 30 minutes. Stir in wine. Heat to boiling; reduce heat. Simmer uncovered, until beef is hot, about 10 minutes. Sprinkle with parsley.

■ *Microwave Directions:* Omit ¼ cup water. Dip container of Beef-Mushroom Mix into very hot water just to loosen. Place frozen block in 3-quart microwaveproof casserole. Cover tightly and microwave on high (100%), stirring occasionally, until hot, 9 to 11 minutes. Stir in wine. Cover and microwave until beef is hot, 4 to 6 minutes. Sprinkle with parsley.

Curried Beef

4 or 5 servings

1	container Beef-Mushroom Mix (left)
¼	cup water
¾	cup cream of coconut
½	teaspoon curry powder
¼	teaspoon chili powder
⅛	teaspoon ground ginger
	Hot cooked rice

Dip container of Beef-Mushroom Mix into very hot water just to loosen. Place frozen block in 3-quart saucepan. Add water. Heat uncovered, over medium heat, stirring occasionally, until hot, about 30 minutes. Stir in cream of coconut, curry powder, chili powder and ginger. Heat to boiling; reduce heat. Simmer uncovered, stirring occasionally, until beef is hot, about 10 minutes. Serve over rice. Garnish with chopped salted peanuts, chopped green onion, chopped green pepper or flaked or shredded coconut if desired.

Beef Stroganoff

4 or 5 servings

1   container Beef-Mushroom Mix (page 16)
¼   cup water
2   tablespoons catsup
½   teaspoon dry mustard
1   cup dairy sour cream
1   tablespoon dry white wine, if desired
    Hot cooked noodles or rice

Dip container of Beef-Mushroom Mix into very hot water just to loosen. Place frozen block in 3-quart saucepan. Add water. Heat uncovered over medium heat, stirring occasionally, until hot, about 30 minutes. Stir in catsup and mustard. Heat to boiling; reduce heat. Simmer uncovered, stirring occasionally, until beef is hot, about 10 minutes. Stir in sour cream and wine; heat just until hot. Serve over noodles. Sprinkle with parsley if desired.

■ *Microwave Directions:* Omit ¼ cup water. Dip container of Beef-Mushroom Mix into very hot water just to loosen. Place frozen block in 3-quart microwaveproof casserole. Cover tightly and microwave on high (100%), stirring occasionally, until hot, 9 to 11 minutes. Stir in catsup and mustard. Cover and microwave until beef is hot, 3 to 5 minutes. Stir in sour cream and wine. Cover and microwave just until hot, 4 to 6 minutes. Serve over noodles. Sprinkle with parsley if desired.

COOKING HAMBURGER PATTIES

Shape 1 pound ground beef into 4 patties, each about 1 inch thick. To fry, cook over medium heat, turning frequently, until desired doneness, about 10 minutes for medium. To broil, place patties on rack in broiler pan. Set oven control to broil and/or 550°. Broil with tops about 3 inches from heat until desired doneness, 5 to 7 minutes on each side. To bake, place patties on rack in broiler pan. Cook in 350° oven until desired doneness, about 30 minutes for medium.

Burgers with Mushrooms and Onions

4 servings

1   pound ground beef
3   tablespoons finely chopped onion
3   tablespoons water
¾   teaspoon salt
⅛   teaspoon pepper
    Mushrooms and Onions (below)

Mix ground beef, onion, water, salt and pepper. Shape mixture into 4 patties, each about ¾ inch thick. Set oven control to broil and/or 550°. Place patties on rack in broiler pan. Broil with tops about 3 inches from heat until desired doneness, 5 to 7 minutes on each side for medium. Prepare Mushrooms and Onions; spoon over hamburgers.

Mushrooms and Onions

1   medium onion, thinly sliced
1   tablespoon margarine or butter
1   can (4 ounces) mushroom stems and pieces,
      drained
½   teaspoon Worcestershire sauce

Cook onion in margarine over medium heat, stirring occasionally, until tender. Stir in mushrooms and Worcestershire sauce; heat until mushrooms are hot.

■ *Microwave Directions:* Prepare ground beef as directed above. Place patties on microwaveproof rack in microwaveproof baking dish. Cover loosely and microwave on high (100%) 3 minutes; rotate dish ½ turn. Microwave until almost done, about 2 minutes longer. Let stand 3 minutes. (Beef will continue to cook while standing.) Place onion and margarine in 1-quart microwaveproof casserole. Cover tightly and microwave on high (100%) until onion is crisp-tender, about 2 minutes. Stir in mushrooms and Worcestershire sauce. Cover tightly and microwave until mushrooms are hot, about 1 minute.

Mini Beef Loaves

6 servings

1   pound ground beef
1   egg
¼   cup milk
2   tablespoons dry bread crumbs
½   teaspoon salt
⅛   teaspoon pepper
1   medium onion, chopped (about ½ cup)
1   small green pepper, chopped (about ½ cup)
¾   cup shredded cheese

Mix ground beef, egg, milk, crumbs, salt and pepper. Press half of the beef mixture in bottoms and halfway up sides of 12 ungreased 2½ × 1¼-inch muffin cups. Fill each with onion, green pepper and cheese. Top with remaining beef mixture, pressing edges to seal. Place muffin pan in ungreased 15½ × 10½ × 1-inch jelly roll pan. Cook uncovered in 350° oven until done, 30 to 35 minutes.

Sour Cream Burgers

4 servings

1   pound ground beef
½   cup dairy sour cream
¼   cup dry bread crumbs
½   envelope (about 1½-ounce size) onion soup mix
        (about 2 tablespoons)
    Dash of pepper

Mix all ingredients. Shape mixture into 4 patties, each about ¾ inch thick. Set oven control to broil and/or 550°. Place patties on rack in broiler pan. Broil with tops about 3 inches from heat until desired doneness, 5 to 7 minutes on each side for medium.

■ *Microwave Directions:* Mix all ingredients. Shape mixture into 4 patties, each about ¾ inch thick. Place patties on microwaveproof rack in microwaveproof baking dish. Cover loosely and microwave on high (100%) 3 minutes; rotate dish ½ turn. Microwave until almost done, about 2 minutes longer. Let stand covered 3 minutes. (Beef will continue to cook while standing.)

Beef and Macaroni

5 servings

1   pound ground beef
1   medium onion, chopped (about ½ cup)
1   cup uncooked elbow macaroni (3 to 4 ounces)
2   cups water
1   small green pepper, chopped (about ½ cup)
1   can (11 ounces) condensed Cheddar cheese
       soup
2   teaspoons Worcestershire sauce
¾   teaspoon salt
⅛   teaspoon pepper
1   package (10 ounces) frozen green peas

Cook and stir ground beef and onion in 10-inch skillet until beef is light brown; drain. Stir in macaroni, water, green pepper, soup, Worcestershire sauce, salt and pepper. Heat to boiling; reduce heat. Cover and simmer, stirring occasionally, 20 minutes. Rinse frozen peas under running cold water to separate; drain. Stir peas into beef mixture. Simmer uncovered until peas and macaroni are tender, about 5 minutes.

■ *Microwave Directions:* Crumble ground beef into 3-quart microwaveproof casserole; add onion. Cover loosely and microwave on high (100%) 3 minutes; break up and stir. Cover and microwave until very little pink remains in beef, 2 to 3 minutes longer; drain. Stir in macaroni, 1¾ cups hot water and the remaining ingredients except peas. Cover tightly and microwave 12 minutes; stir in peas. Cover tightly and microwave until macaroni is almost tender, 5 to 7 minutes longer. Let stand covered 5 minutes.

Skillet Spaghetti

6 servings

1   pound ground beef
1   large onion, chopped (about 1 cup)
1   jar (48 ounces) spaghetti sauce
1   package (7 ounces) thin spaghetti, broken
       into pieces
1   can (4 ounces) mushroom stems and pieces,
       drained
½   cup water
1   tablespoon sugar
½   teaspoon salt
½   cup grated Parmesan cheese

Cook and stir ground beef and onion in 4-quart Dutch oven until beef is light brown; drain. Stir in remaining ingredients except cheese. Heat to boiling; reduce heat. Cover and simmer, stirring occasionally, until spaghetti is tender, about 25 minutes. Sprinkle with cheese.

Oriental Spaghetti

6 servings

1   pound ground beef
1   medium onion, sliced
2   medium stalks celery, sliced (about 1 cup)
1   can (14 ounces) Chinese vegetables, drained
1   can (10¾ ounces) condensed chicken broth
1   package (7 ounces) thin spaghetti, broken
       into pieces
1   can (4 ounces) mushroom stems and pieces,
       drained
1   cup water
2   tablespoons soy sauce
¾   teaspoon ground ginger
¼   teaspoon garlic powder
¼   cup chopped green onions (with tops)

Cook and stir ground beef and onion in 10-inch skillet until beef is light brown; drain. Stir in remaining ingredients except green onions. Heat to boiling; reduce heat. Cover and simmer, stirring occasionally, until spaghetti is tender, about 25 minutes. (A smaller amount water can be added if necessary.) Sprinkle with green onions.

Skillet Stroganoff

5 servings

1   pound ground beef
1   medium onion, chopped (about ½ cup)
1   can (10½ ounces) condensed beef broth
1   can (4 ounces) mushroom stems and pieces, drained
2   cups uncooked egg noodles (about 4 ounces)
1½ cups water
¼   cup catsup
¼   teaspoon garlic powder
1   cup dairy sour cream

Cook and stir ground beef and onion in 10-inch skillet until beef is light brown; drain. Stir in broth, mushrooms, noodles, water, catsup and garlic powder. Heat to boiling; reduce heat. Cover and simmer, stirring occasionally, until noodles are tender, about 30 minutes. (A small amount water can be added if necessary.) Stir in sour cream; heat just until hot.

Beef and Vegetables

6 servings

1   pound ground beef
1   large onion, sliced
1   package (10 ounces) frozen chopped broccoli
2   medium carrots, cut diagonally into ¼-inch slices
1   can (4 ounces) mushroom stems and pieces
1   can (10½ ounces) condensed beef broth
¼   teaspoon ground ginger
¼   teaspoon ground mace
¼   cup soy sauce
1   tablespoon plus 1½ teaspoons cornstarch

Cook and stir ground beef and onion in 10-inch skillet until beef is light brown; drain. Rinse frozen broccoli in cold water to separate; drain. Stir broccoli, carrots, mushrooms (with liquid), broth, ginger and mace into beef mixture. Heat to boiling; reduce heat. Cover and simmer until vegetables are crisp-tender, 5 to 7 minutes. Mix soy sauce and cornstarch; stir into beef mixture. Heat to boiling; reduce heat. Simmer uncovered 1 minute. Serve with hot cooked rice or noodles if desired.

Easy Taco Dinner

Easy Taco Dinner

6 servings

1   pound ground beef
1   large onion, chopped (about 1 cup)
1   envelope (about 1¼ ounces) taco seasoning mix
1   cup water
1   package (12 ounces) tortilla chips
½   head lettuce, shredded
2   medium tomatoes, chopped
1   can (2¼ ounces) sliced ripe olives, drained
1   cup shredded Cheddar or Monterey Jack cheese (about 4 ounces)
⅔   cup dairy sour cream

Cook and stir ground beef and onion in 10-inch skillet until beef is light brown; drain. Stir in seasoning mix and water. Heat to boiling; reduce heat. Simmer uncovered, stirring occasionally, 10 minutes. Spoon beef mixture onto chips. Top with remaining ingredients.

Spaghetti Sauce

3 meals - 6 servings each

3   pounds ground beef
2   large onions, chopped (about 2 cups)
4   cloves garlic, crushed
¼   cup olive oil or vegetable oil
1   cup water
2   cans (28 ounces) whole tomatoes
1   can (12 ounces) tomato paste
2   tablespoons parsley flakes
1   tablespoon sugar
1   tablespoon dried oregano leaves
1   tablespoon dried basil leaves
2   teaspoons salt
1   teaspoon dried marjoram leaves
1   teaspoon pepper

Have ready at serving time for each container:

4   cups hot cooked spaghetti

Cook and stir ground beef, onions and garlic in oil in 4-quart Dutch oven until beef is light brown; drain. Stir in water, tomatoes, tomato paste and seasonings; break up tomatoes with fork. Heat to boiling; reduce heat. Cover and simmer, stirring occasionally, 1 hour. Uncover and simmer until thickened, about 30 minutes. (To serve immediately, serve ⅓ of the Spaghetti Sauce [about 3½ cups] over hot cooked spaghetti.) Divide sauce (about 3½ cups each) among three 1-quart freezer containers. Refrigerate until cool. Cover, label and freeze no longer than 4 months.

TO SERVE: About 40 minutes before serving, dip 1 container Spaghetti Sauce into very hot water just to loosen. Place frozen block in 3-quart saucepan. Cover and heat over medium heat, turning occasionally, until thawed, 20 to 30 minutes. Reduce heat; simmer uncovered 10 minutes. Serve over spaghetti. Sprinkle with grated Parmesan cheese if desired.

■ *Microwave Reheat Directions:* Dip 1 container frozen Spaghetti Sauce into very hot water just to loosen. Place frozen block in 3-quart microwaveproof casserole. Cover tightly and microwave on high (100%), turning occasionally, until thawed, 16 to 20 minutes; stir. Cover and microwave until hot, 5 to 7 minutes longer.

Tamale Pie

2 meals - 6 servings each

2   pounds ground beef
1   large onion, chopped (about 1 cup)
1   can (28 ounces) whole tomatoes, drained
1   package (16 ounces) frozen whole kernel corn
2   cans (4¼ ounces each) chopped ripe olives, drained
2   cans (4 ounces each) chopped green chilies, drained
2   tablespoons chili powder
1   teaspoon garlic powder
1   teaspoon salt
2   cups cornmeal
2   cups milk
¼   cup sugar
4   eggs

Have ready at serving time for each pie:

1   cup shredded Cheddar cheese (about 4 ounces)

Cook and stir ground beef and onion in 4-quart Dutch oven until beef is light brown; drain. Stir in tomatoes, corn, olives, chilies, chili powder, garlic powder and salt; break up tomatoes with fork. Heat to boiling; reduce heat. Simmer uncovered until thickened, about 10 minutes.

Divide beef mixture between 2 ungreased 9 × 9 × 2-inch baking pans. Mix cornmeal, milk, sugar and eggs; spread over beef mixture in pans. (To serve 1 pan immediately, sprinkle cheese over cornmeal mixture. Cook uncovered in 350° oven until golden brown, 40 to 50 minutes.) Wrap, label and freeze no longer than 4 months.

TO SERVE: About 1 hour 20 minutes before serving, remove 1 pan Tamale Pie from freezer and unwrap. Cook uncovered in 400° oven until golden brown and center is hot, about 1¼ hours. Sprinkle with cheese. Cook until cheese is melted, about 5 minutes longer.

Pizza Casserole

2 meals - 6 servings each

2   pounds ground beef
2   large onions, chopped (about 2 cups)
2   cans (28 ounces each) whole tomatoes
1   can (15 ounces) tomato sauce
2   teaspoons Italian seasoning
1½   teaspoons salt
¼   teaspoon pepper
2   packages (5 ounces each) spiral macaroni
2   cups shredded mozzarella cheese
     (about 8 ounces)
½   cup grated Parmesan cheese

Cook and stir ground beef and onions in 4-quart Dutch oven until beef is light brown; drain. Stir in tomatoes (with liquid), tomato sauce, Italian seasoning, salt and pepper; break up tomatoes with fork. Heat to boiling; reduce heat. Simmer uncovered, stirring occasionally, 10 minutes.

Cook macaroni as directed on package; drain. Stir macaroni into beef mixture. Divide mixture between 2 ungreased 8×8×2-inch baking pans. Sprinkle each pan with 1 cup mozzarella cheese and ¼ cup Parmesan cheese. (To serve 1 pan immediately, cook uncovered in 350° oven until hot and golden brown, about 30 minutes.) Wrap, label and freeze no longer than 1 month.

TO SERVE: About 1½ hours before serving, remove 1 pan Pizza Casserole from freezer and unwrap. Cook uncovered in 375° oven until hot and golden brown, about 1½ hours.

Beef and Corn Dinners

4 servings

1   pound ground beef
1   small onion, chopped (about ¼ cup)
1   can (16 ounces) whole kernel corn, drained
1   can (10¾ ounces) condensed cream of
     chicken soup
¼   cup water

Have ready at serving time:

1   can (3 ounces) French fried onions

Cook and stir ground beef and onion in 10-inch skillet until beef is light brown; drain. Stir in corn, soup and water. (To serve immediately, heat until hot; sprinkle with onions.) Divide mixture among four 12-inch squares of heavy-duty or double thickness aluminum foil. Wrap, label and freeze no longer than 2 months.

TO SERVE: About 50 minutes before serving, place frozen Beef and Corn Dinners, seam sides up, on ungreased cookie sheet. Heat on center rack in 450° oven until hot, 40 to 45 minutes. Open each packet; sprinkle with onions.

■ *Microwave Reheat Directions:* Remove Beef and Corn Dinners from freezer and unwrap. Place each frozen dinner in individual microwaveproof dish. Cover tightly and microwave on high (100%), stirring once, until hot, 1 dinner 5 to 7 minutes; 2 dinners 8 to 10 minutes; 3 dinners 10 to 12 minutes; 4 dinners 12 to 14 minutes. Sprinkle each with onions.

PASTA SHAPES

Egg Noodles · Elbow · Ziti · Spiral · Shell · Lasagna · Fettuccine · Linguine · Rigatoni · Spaghetti

Beef-Macaroni Dinners

4 servings

1 cup uncooked elbow macaroni (3 to 4 ounces)
1 pound ground beef
1 medium onion, chopped (about 1/2 cup)
1 can (10 3/4 ounces) condensed tomato soup
1 can (16 ounces) green beans, drained
1/3 cup water
1/8 teaspoon pepper

Have ready at serving time:

1/4 cup grated Parmesan cheese
Snipped parsley

Cook macaroni as directed on package; drain. Cook and stir ground beef and onion in 10-inch skillet until beef is light brown; drain. Stir in macaroni, soup, beans, water and pepper. (To serve immediately, heat until hot. Sprinkle with cheese and parsley.) Divide mixture among four 12-inch squares of heavy-duty or double thickness aluminum foil. Wrap securely, label and freeze no longer than 2 months.

TO SERVE: About 50 minutes before serving, place frozen Beef-Macaroni Dinners, seam sides up, on ungreased cookie sheet. Heat on center rack in 450° oven until hot, 40 to 45 minutes. Open each packet; sprinkle with cheese and parsley.

■ *Microwave Reheat Directions:* Remove Beef-Macaroni Dinners from freezer and unwrap. Place each frozen dinner in individual microwaveproof dish. Cover tightly and microwave on high (100%), stirring once, until hot, 1 dinner 5 to 7 minutes; 2 dinners 8 to 10 minutes; 3 dinners 10 to 12 minutes; 4 dinners 12 to 14 minutes. Sprinkle each with cheese and parsley.

Freezer Ground Beef Mix

3 meals - 6 to 8 servings each

3 pounds ground beef
2 large onions, chopped (about 2 cups)
1 pound mushrooms, sliced, or 1 can (8 ounces) mushroom stems and pieces, drained
2 cloves garlic, finely chopped
2 teaspoons salt
1/2 teaspoon pepper

Cook and stir ground beef, onions, mushrooms and garlic in 4-quart Dutch oven until beef is brown; drain. Stir in salt and pepper. Spread beef mixture in ungreased 15 1/2 × 10 1/2 × 1-inch jelly roll pan. Freeze uncovered 1 hour. (Partial freezing helps prevent beef from freezing together solidly.)

Divide beef mixture (about 3 cups each) among three 1-quart freezer containers. Cover, label and freeze no longer than 3 months. Use Freezer Ground Beef Mix for Cheeseburger Pie (below), Chili Beef Salads (page 25) or Tortilla Beef Dinner (page 25).

Cheeseburger Pie

8 servings

1 container Freezer Ground Beef Mix (above)
1 cup shredded Cheddar cheese (about 4 ounces)
1 1/2 cups milk
3/4 cup Basic Baking Mix (page 105) or buttermilk baking mix
3 eggs
1/2 teaspoon caraway seed, if desired

Heat oven to 400°. Spread Freezer Ground Beef Mix in lightly greased 10 × 1 1/2-inch pie plate; sprinkle with cheese. Beat remaining ingredients with hand beater until smooth. Pour over cheese. Cook until brown and knife inserted in center comes out clean, 30 to 35 minutes. Let stand 5 minutes before cutting.

Chili Beef Salads

6 servings

1   container Freezer Ground Beef Mix (page 23)
¼   cup water
¼   cup chili sauce
1   small head lettuce,* cut crosswise into
     six ½-inch slices
2   medium tomatoes, sliced
     Horseradish Dressing (below)
1   cup alfalfa sprouts
1   avocado, sliced

Heat Freezer Ground Beef Mix, water and chili sauce in 2-quart saucepan over medium heat, stirring occasionally, until beef is hot, about 10 minutes. Spoon beef mixture over lettuce slices on 6 plates. Arrange tomato slices on beef mixture. Spoon Horseradish Dressing over top. Sprinkle with alfalfa sprouts. Arrange avocado slices around salads.

*Lettuce cups with shredded lettuce can be substituted for the lettuce slices.

Horseradish Dressing

½   cup plain yogurt
1   tablespoon prepared mustard
1   teaspoon prepared horseradish
1   teaspoon parsley flakes, if desired

Mix all ingredients.

■ *Microwave Directions:* Place Freezer Ground Beef Mix, water and chili sauce in 2-quart microwaveproof casserole. Cover tightly and microwave on high (100%), stirring once, until beef is hot, 6 to 8 minutes. Continue as directed above.

Tortilla Beef Dinner

6 servings

6   corn tortillas (6 inches in diameter)
⅓   cup vegetable oil
1   container Freezer Ground Beef Mix (page 23)
2   medium tomatoes, chopped (about 2 cups)
½   teaspoon dried oregano leaves
1   cup shredded Cheddar cheese (about 4 ounces)

Cut tortillas into thin strips. Heat oil in 10-inch skillet over medium heat until hot. Cook and stir tortilla strips in oil until crisp. Remove from skillet with slotted spoon; drain on paper towels and reserve. Mix Freezer Ground Beef Mix, tomatoes and oregano in same skillet. Cook and stir until beef is hot, about 10 minutes. Top with tortilla strips; sprinkle with cheese. Cover and heat just until cheese is melted. Serve with sour cream if desired.

■ *Microwave Directions:* Place tortilla strips and 2 tablespoons oil in 2-quart microwaveproof casserole. Microwave uncovered on high (100%) 3 minutes; stir. Microwave until strips are crisp, 3 to 4 minutes longer. Remove from casserole with slotted spoon; drain on paper towels and reserve. Mix Freezer Ground Beef Mix, tomatoes and oregano in same casserole. Cover tightly and microwave 3 minutes; stir. Cover and microwave until beef is hot, 3 to 4 minutes longer. Top with tortilla strips; sprinkle with cheese. Microwave uncovered until cheese is melted, 2 to 4 minutes. Serve with sour cream if desired.

DINNER IN A HURRY

Tortilla Beef Dinner (above)

Buttered Corn

Avocado-Orange Salad

Toasted Cake Toppers (page 139)

Freezer Beef Squares

3 meals - 5 to 6 servings each

3   pounds ground beef
3   eggs, slightly beaten
1½ cups dry bread crumbs
1   envelope (about 1½ ounces) onion soup mix
¾   cup milk

Mix all ingredients. Pat mixture into rectangle, 15×9 inches, in ungreased 15½×10½ ×1-inch jelly roll pan. Cut into 1½-inch squares; separate squares slightly.

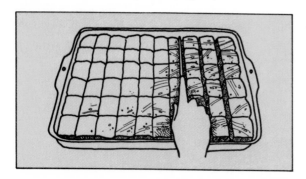

Cook uncovered in 400° oven until brown, 25 to 30 minutes. Cool 5 minutes. Freeze uncovered 15 minutes. (This partial freezing keeps squares from freezing together solidly.)

Divide squares among three 1-quart freezer containers. Cover, label and freeze no longer than 2 months. Use Freezer Beef Squares in Beef Rarebit (right), Beef Provençale (page 27) or Beef Skillet Dinner (page 27).

Beef Rarebit

6 servings

¾   cup beer
2   cups shredded sharp process American cheese
     (about 8 ounces)
½   teaspoon dry mustard
¼   teaspoon Worcestershire sauce
⅛   teaspoon cayenne pepper
1   container Freezer Beef Squares (left)
     Paprika or snipped parsley

Heat beer just to boiling in 3-quart saucepan. Stir in cheese, mustard, Worcestershire sauce and cayenne. Heat, stirring constantly, until cheese is melted. Break Freezer Beef Squares apart; stir into cheese mixture. Heat to boiling; reduce heat. Simmer uncovered, stirring occasionally, until beef squares are hot, 15 to 18 minutes. Sprinkle with paprika. Serve over hot cooked noodles if desired.

☐ *Microwave Directions:* Microwave ⅔ cup beer uncovered in 2-quart microwaveproof casserole on high (100%) until boiling, about 2 minutes. Stir in cheese, mustard, Worcestershire sauce and cayenne. Microwave uncovered until cheese is melted, 2 to 4 minutes; stir until smooth. Break Freezer Beef Squares apart; stir into cheese mixture. Cover and microwave until thawed, 5 to 7 minutes; stir. Cover and microwave until beef squares are hot, 3 to 5 minutes longer. Sprinkle with paprika. Serve over hot cooked noodles if desired.

Beef Provençale

5 servings

1   can (16 ounces) stewed tomatoes
½   teaspoon garlic powder
1   container Freezer Beef Squares (page 26)
2   small zucchini, cut into ½-inch slices
½   cup pitted ripe olives
¼   cup grated Parmesan cheese

Heat tomatoes and garlic powder to boiling in 3-quart saucepan. Break Freezer Beef Squares apart; stir into tomato mixture. Heat to boiling; reduce heat. Cover and simmer until beef squares are hot, about 10 minutes. Stir in zucchini and olives. Heat to boiling; reduce heat. Cover and simmer until zucchini is crisp-tender, about 10 minutes. Sprinkle with cheese.

Microwave Directions: Place tomatoes and garlic powder in 2-quart microwaveproof casserole. Cover tightly and microwave on high (100%) until boiling, 5 to 7 minutes. Break Freezer Beef Squares apart; stir into tomato mixture. Cover and microwave until beef squares are thawed, about 4 minutes. Stir in zucchini and olives. Cover and microwave until zucchini is crisp-tender, 4 to 6 minutes. Sprinkle with cheese.

Beef Skillet Dinner

5 servings

1   can (10¾ ounces) condensed golden mushroom soup
1   cup water
1   container Freezer Beef Squares (page 26)
1   package (10 ounces) frozen San Francisco-style vegetables

Mix soup and water in 10-inch skillet. Break Freezer Beef Squares apart; stir into soup mixture. Heat to boiling; reduce heat. Cover and simmer until beef squares are hot, about 10 minutes. Rinse frozen vegetables in cold water to separate; drain. Reserve topping packet. Sprinkle vegetables over beef mixture. Heat to boiling; reduce heat. Cover and simmer until vegetables are tender, about 5 minutes. Sprinkle with reserved topping.

Microwave Directions: Mix soup and ¾ cup water in 3-quart microwaveproof casserole. Cover tightly and microwave on high (100%) 2 minutes. Break Freezer Beef Squares apart; stir into soup mixture. Cover and microwave until thawed, 5 to 7 minutes. Rinse frozen vegetables under running cold water to separate; drain. Reserve topping packet. Sprinkle vegetables over beef mixture. Cover and microwave until vegetables are tender, 3 to 5 minutes. Sprinkle with reserved topping.

Fruited Pork Chops

4 servings

4   *pork loin or rib chops (about ½ inch thick)*
1   *can (8¼ ounces) pineapple chunks, drained*
1   *cup pitted prunes*
½   *cup dried apricots*
½   *cup bottled sweet-and-spicy French salad
     dressing*

Cook pork over medium heat until brown; drain. Place pineapple, prunes and apricots on pork. Pour dressing over fruit and pork. Heat to boiling; reduce heat. Cover and simmer until pork is done, 20 to 25 minutes.

Italian Pork Steak

6 servings

½   *pound link Italian sausage, cut into ½-inch
     slices*
3   *pork blade steaks (about ½ inch thick),
     cut into halves*
1   *can (8 ounces) stewed tomatoes*
1   *can (4 ounces) mushroom stems and pieces,
     drained*
1   *medium onion, sliced and separated into rings*

Cook and stir sausage in 10-inch skillet until brown; remove sausage and reserve. Cook pork in same skillet over medium heat until brown; drain. Add tomatoes, mushrooms, onion and reserved sausage. Heat to boiling; reduce heat. Cover and simmer until pork is done, 20 to 25 minutes.

■ *Microwave Directions:* Arrange pork in microwaveproof dish, 12 × 7½ × 2 inches, with meaty edges to outsides. Place sausage on pork. Cover tightly and microwave on medium (50%) 15 minutes, rotating dish ¼ turn every 5 minutes; drain. Layer onion, mushrooms and tomatoes on meat. Cover and microwave, rotating dish ¼ turn every 5 minutes, until pork is done (170° on meat thermometer), 15 to 20 minutes. Let stand covered 5 minutes.

Pork Chops in Raisin Sauce

4 servings

4   *pork loin or rib chops (about ½ inch thick)*
2   *small cloves garlic, thinly sliced*
1   *teaspoon salt*
¼   *teaspoon pepper*
¾   *cup raisins*
1   *can (16 ounces) stewed tomatoes*
1   *or 2 pickled chili peppers, chopped*

Make small cuts in each pork chop with sharp knife; insert slice of garlic in each cut. Cook pork in 10-inch skillet over medium heat until brown; drain. Sprinkle with salt and pepper. Add remaining ingredients. Heat to boiling; reduce heat. Cover and simmer until pork is done, 25 to 30 minutes.

Pork Chops with Kiwi Sauce

4 servings

4   *pork loin or rib chops (about ½ inch thick)*
½   *teaspoon salt*
½   *cup dry white wine or apple juice*
2   *tablespoons packed brown sugar*
2   *tablespoons lime juice*
1   *teaspoon cornstarch*
¼   *cup cold water*
1   *kiwi, peeled and sliced*

Cook pork in 10-inch skillet over medium heat until brown; drain. Sprinkle with salt. Mix wine, brown sugar and lime juice; pour over pork. Heat to boiling; reduce heat. Cover and simmer until pork is done, 20 to 25 minutes. Remove pork to warm platter; keep warm. Mix cornstarch and water; gradually stir into skillet. Heat to boiling, stirring constantly. Boil and stir 1 minute. Stir in kiwi; pour over pork.

BROILING PORK CHOPS OR STEAKS

Slash outer edge of fat at 1-inch intervals to prevent curling (do not cut into lean). Place pork on rack in broiler pan. Set oven control to broil and/or 550°. Broil until light brown or about half done. Sprinkle brown side with salt and pepper if desired. Turn pork; broil until brown and done.

Approximate Total Cooking Time		
Thickness	From Heat	Minutes
½ to ¾ inch	3 to 5 inches	20 to 22
¾ to 1 inch	3 to 5 inches	20 to 25

Pork Scallopini

6 servings

1½ pounds pork tenderloin
2 eggs, slightly beaten
2 tablespoons water
1½ cups finely crushed cracker crumbs
        (about 30 crackers)
⅛ teaspoon garlic powder
⅛ teaspoon onion powder
⅛ teaspoon pepper
3 tablespoons margarine or butter
1 cup dry white wine
2 tablespoons margarine or butter
1 teaspoon cornstarch
1 tablespoon cold water
1 tablespoon snipped parsley

Remove excess fat; cut pork diagonally into ½-inch slices. Mix eggs and 2 tablespoons water. Mix crumbs, garlic powder, onion powder and pepper. Toss pork with egg mixture; coat with crumb mixture. Heat 3 tablespoons margarine in 12-inch skillet over medium heat until hot. Cook half of the pork at a time in margarine until done, about 12 minutes. (Add more margarine if necessary.) Remove pork from skillet; keep warm. Stir wine and 2 tablespoons margarine into skillet. Heat to boiling. Mix cornstarch and 1 tablespoon water; stir into wine mixture. Cook and stir 1 minute. Pour over pork; sprinkle with parsley. Serve with lemon slices if desired.

Pizza

2 pizzas

1 pound bulk Italian sausage
    Pizza Dough* (below)
2 cans (16 ounces each) whole tomatoes,
        drained
1 large onion, chopped
2 teaspoons dried oregano leaves
½ teaspoon garlic powder
1 large green pepper, chopped (about 1½ cups)
1 can (8 ounces) mushroom stems and pieces,
        drained and coarsely chopped
2 cups shredded mozzarella cheese
        (about 8 ounces)

Cook and stir sausage until light brown; drain. Prepare Pizza Dough. Mix tomatoes, onion, oregano and garlic powder; break up tomatoes with fork. Divide dough into halves. Pat each half into 10½-inch circle on lightly greased cookie sheet with floured fingers. Spread tomato mixture over circles. Sprinkle with sausage and the remaining ingredients. Bake in 425° oven until cheese is light brown, 20 to 25 minutes.

*Two 10½-inch ready-to-bake pizza crusts can be substituted for the Pizza Dough.

Pizza Dough

1 package active dry yeast
1 cup warm water (105° to 115°)
2½ cups all-purpose flour
2 tablespoons vegetable oil
1 teaspoon sugar
1 teaspoon salt

Dissolve yeast in warm water in 3-quart bowl. Stir in remaining ingredients; beat vigorously 20 strokes. Let rest about 5 minutes.

Ham Slice with Rice

6 servings

1½ - pound fully cooked smoked ham slice
    (1 inch thick)
  1 cup dairy sour cream
  2 tablespoons Dijon-style mustard
  3 cups hot cooked rice
  ½ cup raisins
  ⅓ cup sliced green onions (with tops)

Place ham in center of ungreased 13 × 9 × 2-inch baking dish. Mix sour cream and mustard in 2-quart bowl; stir in rice, raisins and onions. Spoon rice mixture around ham. Cover and cook in 325° oven 15 minutes. Uncover and cook until hot, 10 to 15 minutes longer.

■ *Microwave Directions:* Place ham in 12 × 7½ × 2-inch microwaveproof dish. Prepare rice mixture as directed above; spoon around ham. Cover tightly and microwave on medium-high (70%) 5 minutes; rotate dish ½ turn. Microwave until hot, 4 to 6 minutes longer.

Upside-down Pancake

Ham and Zucchini Skillet

6 servings

  1 medium onion, thinly sliced
  2 tablespoons margarine or butter
  3 cups cut-up fully cooked smoked ham
  4 small zucchini (about 1 pound),
        cut into ¼-inch strips
  1 green pepper, cut into ¼-inch slices
  ⅛ teaspoon pepper
  ½ cup dairy sour cream
  1 teaspoon poppy seed

Cook and stir onion in margarine in 10-inch skillet until tender. Stir in ham, zucchini, green pepper and pepper. Cover and cook over medium heat, stirring occasionally, until vegetables are crisp-tender, about 8 minutes. Stir in sour cream and poppy seed; heat just until hot. Serve with hot cooked rice or noodles if desired.

Upside-down Pancake

4 servings

  ¾ pound Canadian-style bacon, sliced
  1 cup maple-flavored syrup
  2 eggs
1½ cups all-purpose flour
1½ cups milk
  ¼ cup margarine or butter, melted
  1 tablespoon plus 1½ teaspoons baking powder
  1 tablespoon sugar
  ½ teaspoon salt
  1 jar (15 ounces) chunky applesauce

Arrange bacon slices, overlapping slightly, in ungreased 13 × 9 × 2-inch baking dish. Pour syrup over bacon. Beat eggs in 1-quart bowl with hand beater until foamy; beat in remaining ingredients except applesauce just until smooth. Pour over bacon and syrup. Bake uncovered in 400° oven until golden brown and firm, 20 to 25 minutes. Heat applesauce just until warm. Cut pancake into 8 pieces; invert on serving plates. Serve with applesauce.

Spaghetti with Franks

5 servings

1   package (16 ounces) frankfurters,
      cut diagonally into 1-inch pieces
1   medium onion, chopped (about ½ cup)
1   small green pepper, chopped (about ½ cup)
1   tablespoon margarine or butter
1   can (26 ounces) spaghettios in tomato and
      cheese sauce
3   slices process American cheese, cut diagonally
      into halves

Cook and stir frankfurters, onion and green pepper in margarine in 10-inch skillet until onion is tender. Stir in spaghettios. Heat to boiling, stirring occasionally; reduce heat. Arrange cheese on top. Cover and simmer until cheese is melted, 3 to 5 minutes.

■ *Microwave Directions:* Place frankfurters, onion, green pepper and margarine in 2-quart microwaveproof casserole. Cover with paper towel and microwave on high (100%) 3 minutes. Stir in spaghettios. Cover tightly and microwave until hot, 5 to 7 minutes. Arrange cheese on top. Cover and let stand until cheese is melted, about 3 minutes.

Pork and Sauerkraut

4 servings

1   can (12 ounces) pork luncheon meat,
      cut lengthwise into 4 slices
1   can (16 ounces) sauerkraut, drained
1   can or bottle (12 ounces) beer

Cook pork in 10-inch skillet over medium heat until light brown, about 5 minutes. Spoon sauerkraut on top and around pork; pour beer over sauerkraut. Heat to boiling; reduce heat. Simmer uncovered until liquid is almost absorbed, about 30 minutes.

Braised Pork and Vegetables

6 to 8 servings

3½ - to 4-pound pork shoulder roast
  2   tablespoons vegetable oil
  1   tablespoon instant chicken bouillon
  1   teaspoon garlic powder
1½   cups water

Have ready at serving time:

1   can (14 ounces) artichoke hearts, drained
1   large tomato, cut into wedges
2   medium green peppers, cut into rings
1   large onion, sliced and separated into rings

Cook pork in oil in 4-quart Dutch oven over medium heat, turning occasionally, until brown; drain. Add instant bouillon, garlic powder and water. Heat to boiling; reduce heat. Cover and simmer until pork is done, about 3 hours. (To serve immediately, skim fat from broth. Add artichoke hearts, tomatoes, green peppers and onion. Heat to boiling; reduce heat. Cover and simmer until green peppers and onion are crisp-tender, about 5 minutes. Remove pork and vegetables to warm platter; keep warm. Skim fat from broth. Heat broth to boiling; boil until reduced to about 1½ cups, 5 to 10 minutes. Serve broth with pork.) Cover and refrigerate pork and broth separately. Store no longer than 48 hours.

TO SERVE: About 1 hour before serving, remove fat from broth. Heat pork and broth to boiling; reduce heat. Cover and simmer until pork is hot, about 30 minutes. Add artichoke hearts, tomatoes, green peppers and onion. Heat to boiling; reduce heat. Cover and simmer until green pepper and onion are crisp-tender, about 5 minutes. Remove pork and vegetables to warm platter; keep warm. Skim fat from broth. Heat broth to boiling; boil until reduced to about 1½ cups, 5 to 10 minutes. Serve broth with pork.

Pork and Dumplings

6 servings

1   medium onion, thinly sliced
1   small green pepper, cut into thin strips
2   tablespoons margarine or butter
2½   cups cut-up cooked pork
1   cup water
1   can (16 ounces) whole kernel corn, drained
1   can (10¾ ounces) condensed cream of
       chicken soup
1   jar (2 ounces) diced pimiento, drained
       Dumplings (below)

Cook and stir onion and green pepper in margarine in 10-inch skillet until onion is tender. Stir in pork, water, corn, soup and pimiento. Heat to boiling; reduce heat. Prepare Dumplings; drop by spoonfuls onto hot pork mixture. Cook uncovered over low heat 10 minutes. Cover and cook until dumplings are done, about 10 minutes longer.

Dumplings

Mix 2 cups Basic Baking Mix* (page 105) and ¾ cup milk until soft dough forms.

CHEESE DUMPLINGS: Mix in 1 cup shredded Cheddar or process American cheese and 1 tablespoon finely chopped onion.

CHILI DUMPLINGS: Mix in ¼ cup chopped green onions and 1 teaspoon chili powder.

DILL DUMPLINGS: Mix in 1 teaspoon dried dill weed and ¼ teaspoon grated lemon peel.

EGG DUMPLINGS: Decrease milk to ⅓ cup. Mix in 2 eggs, slightly beaten, and 2 tablespoons snipped parsley.

HERB DUMPLINGS: Mix in 1 tablespoon parsley flakes, 1 teaspoon poultry seasoning and 1 teaspoon instant minced onion.

*2 cups buttermilk baking mix can be substituted for the Basic Baking Mix. Decrease milk to ⅔ cup.

Barbecued Pork

6 servings

4   cups cut-up cooked pork
1   large onion, sliced
2   cups barbecue sauce

Cook and stir pork and onion in 3-quart saucepan over medium heat until onion is tender, about 10 minutes. Stir in barbecue sauce; heat until pork mixture is hot, about 5 minutes. Serve over hot cooked rice, spaghetti or noodles if desired.

Barbecued Country-Style Ribs

6 to 8 servings

3   pounds pork country-style ribs
⅔   cup chili sauce
½   cup grape jelly
1   tablespoon dry red wine
1   teaspoon Dijon-style mustard

Cut pork into serving pieces if necessary. Arrange pork, meaty sides up, in ungreased 13 × 9 × 2-inch baking pan. Cover and cook in 325° oven until tender, about 1½ hours; drain. Heat remaining ingredients, stirring occasionally, until jelly is melted. Pour over ribs. (To serve immediately, continue as directed in TO SERVE except — cook about 30 minutes.) Cover and refrigerate no longer than 48 hours.

TO SERVE: About 45 minutes before serving, cook uncovered in 325° oven, spooning sauce over top occasionally, until pork is hot and glazed, about 40 minutes. Serve sauce over pork.

■ *Pressure Cooker Directions:* Cut pork into serving pieces if necessary. Place pork and 1 cup water in 6-quart pressure cooker. Following manufacturer's directions, cover and cook at 15 pounds pressure 15 minutes. Cool 5 minutes; reduce pressure. Transfer pork to ungreased 13 × 9 × 2-inch baking pan. Heat remaining ingredients, stirring occasionally, until jelly is melted. Pour over ribs. Continue as directed in TO SERVE except — cook about 30 minutes.

Freezer Pork Cubes

3 meals - 6 servings each

4½ pounds pork boneless shoulder, cut into 1-inch cubes
2   teaspoons salt
1   teaspoon dried thyme leaves
½   teaspoon garlic powder
½   teaspoon onion powder
¼   teaspoon pepper
2   cups water

Cook and stir pork in 12-inch skillet or 4-quart Dutch oven over medium heat until brown, about 20 minutes. Sprinkle with salt, thyme, garlic powder, onion powder and pepper; stir in water. Heat to boiling; reduce heat. Cover and simmer until pork is done, 1 to 1¼ hours. Drain pork; arrange in single layer in ungreased 15½ × 10½ × 1-inch jelly roll pan. Freeze uncovered 30 minutes. (This partial freezing prevents pork from freezing together solidly.)

Divide pork (about 2 cups) among three 1-pint freezer containers. Cover, label and freeze no longer than 2 months. Use in Pork and Hominy (below), Pork and Cabbage (right) or Sweet-and-Sour Pork (right).

Pork and Hominy

6 servings

1   medium onion, chopped (about ½ cup)
2   tablespoons margarine or butter
1   container Freezer Pork Cubes (above)
1   can (20 ounces) hominy, drained
1   can (4 ounces) chopped green chilies, drained
2   medium tomatoes, chopped (about 1½ cups)
1   teaspoon chili powder
¾   cup shredded Cheddar cheese

Cook and stir onion in margarine in 10-inch skillet over medium heat until tender. Stir in Freezer Pork Cubes, hominy, chilies, tomatoes and chili powder. Cover and cook, stirring occasionally, until pork is hot, about 10 minutes. Sprinkle with cheese; cover and cook until cheese is melted, about 5 minutes.

Pork and Cabbage

6 servings

1   container Freezer Pork Cubes (left)
1   large onion, sliced
1   cup water
2   tablespoons paprika
1   tablespoon instant chicken bouillon
1   teaspoon salt
⅛   teaspoon pepper
1   small head cabbage, thinly sliced
1   can (16 ounces) sliced carrots, drained
1   teaspoon caraway seed, if desired
½   cup dairy sour cream

Heat Freezer Pork Cubes, onion, water, paprika, bouillon, salt and pepper in Dutch oven over medium heat, stirring occasionally, until pork is hot, about 10 minutes. Add cabbage, carrots and caraway seed. Heat to boiling; reduce heat. Simmer uncovered just until cabbage is tender, 10 minutes. Stir in sour cream.

Sweet-and-Sour Pork

6 servings

1   container Freezer Pork Cubes (left)
⅔   cup water
½   cup sugar
½   cup white vinegar
1   tablespoon instant chicken bouillon
2   tablespoons soy sauce
2   tablespoons cornstarch
2   tablespoons cold water
2   medium tomatoes, each cut into 6 wedges
1   medium green pepper, cut into 1-inch pieces
2   green onions, cut into 1-inch pieces
1   can (8¼ ounces) pineapple chunks, drained

Heat Freezer Pork Cubes, ⅔ cup water, the sugar, vinegar, instant bouillon and soy sauce to boiling in 3-quart saucepan over medium heat; reduce heat. Cover and simmer, stirring occasionally, until pork is hot, about 10 minutes. Mix cornstarch and 2 tablespoons water; stir into pork mixture. Heat to boiling, stirring constantly. Boil and stir 1 minute. Stir in tomatoes, green pepper, onions and pineapple. Heat to boiling. Serve with rice, if desired.

Lasagna

8 servings

1   *pound bulk Italian sausage or ground beef*
1   *medium onion, chopped (about ½ cup)*
1   *clove garlic, crushed*
1   *can (16 ounces) whole tomatoes*
1   *can (15 ounces) tomato sauce*
2   *tablespoons parsley flakes*
1   *teaspoon sugar*
1   *teaspoon dried basil leaves*
½   *teaspoon salt*
9   *uncooked lasagna noodles (about 8 ounces)*
1   *carton (16 ounces) ricotta or creamed cottage cheese (about 2 cups)*
¼   *cup grated Parmesan cheese*
1   *tablespoon parsley flakes*
1½ *teaspoons salt*
1½ *teaspoons dried oregano leaves*
2   *cups shredded mozzarella cheese (about 8 ounces)*
¼   *cup grated Parmesan cheese*

Cook and stir sausage, onion and garlic in 10-inch skillet until sausage is brown; drain. Add tomatoes (with liquid), tomato sauce, 2 tablespoons parsley, the sugar, basil and ½ teaspoon salt. Heat to boiling, stirring occasionally; reduce heat. Simmer uncovered until consistency of thick spaghetti sauce, about 1 hour.

Cook noodles as directed on package; drain. Reserve ½ cup of the sauce mixture. Mix ricotta cheese, ¼ cup Parmesan cheese, 1 tablespoon parsley, 1½ teaspoons salt and the oregano. Layer ⅓ each of the noodles, remaining sauce mixture, mozzarella cheese and ricotta cheese mixture in ungreased 13 × 9 × 2-inch baking pan. Repeat 2 times. Spoon reserved sauce mixture over top; sprinkle with ¼ cup Parmesan cheese. (To serve immediately, cook uncovered in 350° oven until hot and bubbly, about 45 minutes. Let stand 15 minutes before cutting.) Cover and refrigerate no longer than 24 hours.

TO SERVE: About 1¼ hours before serving, cook Lasagna uncovered in 350° oven until hot, about 55 minutes. Let stand 15 minutes before cutting.

Sausage Kabobs

Sausage Kabobs

4 servings

1   *pound fully cooked kielbasa or smoked sausage, cut into 12 pieces*
1   *jar (16 ounces) small whole onions, drained*
8   *medium mushrooms*
2   *medium zucchini, each cut into 8 pieces*
⅓   *cup orange marmalade*
2   *tablespoons vegetable oil*
1   *tablespoon soy sauce*
1   *teaspoon ground ginger*
½   *teaspoon dry mustard*

Place sausage, onions, mushrooms and zucchini in 2-quart bowl. Mix remaining ingredients; pour over sausage and vegetables. Cover and refrigerate, stirring occasionally, at least 1 hour but no longer than 24 hours.

TO SERVE: About 20 minutes before serving, drain sausage and vegetables, reserving marinade. Alternate sausage and vegetables on 4 metal skewers. Set oven control to broil and/or 550°. Place kabobs on rack in broiler pan. Brush with reserved marinade. Broil with tops 4 inches from heat 6 minutes; turn. Brush with marinade. Broil until sausage is hot and zucchini is crisp-tender, 6 to 8 minutes. Brush with marinade before serving.

Ham and Celery Casserole

6 servings

1   medium onion, chopped (about ½ cup)
⅓   cup whole blanched almonds
2   tablespoons margarine or butter
1   can (10¾ ounces) condensed cream of
      chicken soup
¾   cup milk
3   cups cut-up fully cooked smoked ham
3   medium stalks celery, sliced (about 1½ cups)
4   ounces Swiss cheese, cut into ½-inch cubes

Have ready at serving time:

2   cups corn flakes cereal, coarsely crushed
      (about ⅔ cup)
2   tablespoons margarine or butter, melted
⅛   teaspoon dried dill weed

Cook and stir onion and almonds in 2 tablespoons margarine over medium heat until almonds are golden brown. Mix soup and milk in ungreased 1½-quart casserole. Stir in onion, almonds, ham, celery and cheese. (To serve immediately, toss cereal, 2 tablespoons margarine and the dill weed; sprinkle over ham mixture. Cook uncovered in 350° oven until hot, about 30 minutes.) Cover and refrigerate no longer than 48 hours.

TO SERVE: About 1 hour before serving, toss cereal, 2 tablespoons margarine and the dill weed; sprinkle over Ham and Celery Casserole. Cook uncovered in 350° oven until hot, about 50 minutes.

Ham and Cheese Strudels

8 servings

2   cups finely chopped fully cooked smoked ham
1   cup shredded Swiss cheese (about 4 ounces)
1   can (4 ounces) mushroom stems and pieces,
      drained and chopped
1   egg, slightly beaten
¼   cup sliced green onions (with tops)
8   frozen phyllo leaves, thawed
⅓   cup margarine or butter, melted

Have ready at serving time:

½   cup dairy sour cream
½   cup mayonnaise or salad dressing
2   tablespoons dry mustard
½   teaspoon sugar

Mix ham, cheese, mushrooms, egg and onions. Brush 1 phyllo leaf with margarine. (Keep remaining leaves covered with a dampened towel to prevent them from drying out.) Assemble as pictured at right. (1) Fold leaf crosswise in half; brush with margarine. (2) Fold crosswise in half again; brush with margarine. Place ½ cup ham mixture in center of leaf. (3) Fold long sides up and over filling, overlapping slightly. Fold into thirds from narrow edge. (4) Place strudel, seam side down, on ungreased cookie sheet. (Cover with dampened towel to prevent drying out.) Repeat with remaining phyllo leaves and ham mixture. (To serve immediately, bake strudels uncovered in 350° oven until golden brown, about 35 minutes. Mix sour cream, mayonnaise, mustard and sugar in 1-quart saucepan. Heat over low heat, stirring occasionally, until warm. Serve with strudels.) Wrap plastic wrap over dampened towel and refrigerate no longer than 24 hours.

TO SERVE: About 45 minutes before serving, bake Ham and Cheese Strudels uncovered in 350° oven until golden brown, about 40 minutes. Mix sour cream, mayonnaise, mustard and sugar; heat over low heat, stirring constantly, until warm. Serve with strudels.

BEEF AND CHEESE STRUDELS: Cook and stir 1 pound ground beef until brown; drain. Stir in 1 tablespoon dried dill weed and ¾ teaspoon salt. Substitute beef mixture for the ham.

Ham and Cheese Strudels

How to Assemble Strudels

1.

2.

3.

4.

Minted Pears and Lamb

Veal and Artichokes

4 servings

4   veal cutlets (about 4 ounces each)
2   tablespoons margarine or butter
1   can (10¾ ounces) condensed chicken broth
1   can (14 ounces) artichoke hearts, drained and
    cut into fourths
1   tablespoon capers
1   tablespoon lemon juice
⅛   teaspoon dried dill weed
2   tablespoons cold water
2   teaspoons cornstarch

Cook veal in margarine in 10-inch skillet over medium heat, turning once, until golden. Add broth. Heat to boiling; reduce heat. Cover and simmer until veal is tender, about 10 minutes. Remove veal to warm platter; keep warm. Add enough water to broth mixture in skillet, if necessary, to measure 1 cup. Stir in artichokes, capers, lemon juice and dill weed. Mix water and cornstarch; gradually stir into artichokes. Heat to boiling, stirring constantly. Boil and stir 1 minute. Serve over veal.

Minted Pears and Lamb

6 servings

6   lamb shoulder chops (about ¾ inch thick)
    Salt and pepper
1   can (16 ounces) pear halves, drained
¼   cup margarine or butter, melted
    Juice of 1 large lemon (about ¼ cup)
½   teaspoon dried mint leaves

Diagonally slash outer edge of fat on lamb at 1-inch intervals to prevent curling (do not cut into lean). Set oven control to broil and/or 550°. Place lamb on rack in broiler pan. Broil with tops 2 to 3 inches from heat until brown, about 6 minutes. Sprinkle with salt and pepper; turn. Broil until done, 5 to 7 minutes longer. About 2 minutes before lamb is done, arrange pear halves, cut sides up, around lamb. Mix margarine, lemon juice and mint; brush over pears. Heat remaining margarine mixture; serve with lamb. Fill pears with mint jelly if desired.

BROILING LAMB CHOPS

Remove fell (the paperlike covering) if it is on chops. Slash outer edge of fat at 1-inch intervals to prevent curling (do not cut into lean). Place chops on rack on broiler pan. Set oven control to broil and/or 550°. Broil until brown or about half done. Sprinkle brown side with salt and pepper if desired. Turn chops; broil until brown and desired doneness.

Approximate Total Cooking Time for Medium Doneness		
Thickness	From Heat	Minutes
¾ to 1 inch	2 to 3 inches	12
1½ inches	3 to 5 inches	18
2 inches	3 to 5 inches	22

Lamb Veronique

6 servings

2   pounds lamb boneless shoulder
1/3 cup all-purpose flour
1   teaspoon garlic powder
1   teaspoon paprika
1   teaspoon salt
1   teaspoon ground nutmeg
1/4 teaspoon pepper
1/4 cup vegetable oil
1   medium onion, chopped (about 1/2 cup)
1 1/2 cups water
1/4 cup lemon juice

Have ready at serving time:

1   can (10 3/4 ounces) condensed cream of
        chicken soup
8   ounces mushrooms, sliced, or 1 can (4 ounces)
        mushroom stems and pieces, drained
2   cups seedless green grapes or 1 can
        (16 ounces) grapes, drained

Trim excess fat from lamb. Cut lamb into 2-inch pieces. Mix flour, garlic powder, paprika, salt, nutmeg and pepper. Coat lamb with flour mixture. Heat oil in 10-inch skillet or 4-quart Dutch oven until hot. Cook and stir lamb in oil over medium heat until brown; drain. Add onion, water and lemon juice. Heat to boiling; reduce heat. Cover and simmer until lamb is tender, 1 to 1 1/2 hours. (To serve immediately, continue as directed in TO SERVE.) Cover and refrigerate no longer than 48 hours.

TO SERVE: About 35 minutes before serving, heat lamb mixture to boiling. Stir in soup, mushrooms and grapes. Heat to boiling; reduce heat. Cover and simmer until lamb is hot, about 15 minutes. Serve with hot cooked brown rice or barley if desired.

▪ *Pressure Cooker Directions:* Prepare and coat lamb with flour mixture as directed. Heat oil in 6-quart pressure cooker. Cook and stir lamb in oil until brown; drain. Add onion, water and lemon juice. Following manufacturer's directions, cover and cook at 15 pounds pressure 15 minutes. Cool 5 minutes; reduce pressure. Continue as directed in TO SERVE.

Minted Lamb Shanks

4 servings

4   lamb shanks (about 1 pound each)
2   tablespoons vegetable oil
1   large onion, sliced
1   cup dry white wine
1   tablespoon instant chicken bouillon

Have ready at serving time:

1   tablespoon cornstarch
1   tablespoon cold water
1   cup lemon-flavored yogurt
1   tablespoon snipped fresh mint leaves or
        1 teaspoon dried mint leaves

Cook lamb in oil in 4-quart Dutch oven, turning occasionally, until brown; drain. Add onion, wine and instant bouillon. Heat to boiling; reduce heat. Cover and simmer, turning occasionally, until tender, about 2 hours. (To serve immediately, continue as directed in TO SERVE.) Cover and refrigerate lamb and broth separately. Store no longer than 48 hours.

TO SERVE: About 40 minutes before serving, remove fat from broth. Heat lamb and broth to boiling; reduce heat. Cover and simmer until lamb is hot, about 15 minutes. Remove lamb to warm platter; keep warm. Drain broth, reserving 1 cup in pan. Mix cornstarch and water; gradually stir into broth. Heat to boiling, stirring constantly. Boil and stir 1 minute. Stir in yogurt and mint leaves; heat just until hot. Serve sauce with lamb.

▪ *Pressure Cooker Directions:* Cook 2 lamb shanks at a time in oil in 4-quart pressure cooker, turning occasionally, until brown; drain. Add onion, wine and instant bouillon. Following manufacturer's directions, cover and cook at 15 pounds pressure 35 minutes. Cool 5 minutes; reduce pressure. Remove lamb to warm platter; keep warm. Continue as directed in TO SERVE.

Poultry & Seafood

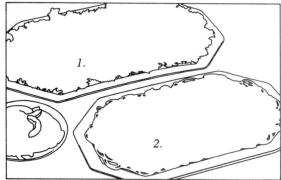

1. Marinated Tarragon Salmon, 2. Chicken Scallopini

Curried Chicken

6 servings

2½ - to 3-pound broiler-fryer chicken, cut up
¼ teaspoon salt
⅛ teaspoon pepper
2 tablespoons vegetable oil
1 small onion, finely chopped
1 large stalk celery, finely chopped
1 large clove garlic, finely chopped
2 tablespoons curry powder
1 medium apple, cut into ½-inch pieces
1 tablespoon catsup
1 can (10¾ ounces) condensed chicken broth
½ cup whipping cream
1 tablespoon cornstarch
1 tablespoon cold water

Cut each chicken breast half into halves. Sprinkle chicken with salt and pepper. Heat oil in 12-inch skillet until hot. Cook chicken, skin sides down, in oil until golden brown, about 5 minutes; turn. Stir in onion, celery and garlic. Cook uncovered over medium heat 2 minutes. Stir in curry powder and apple; cook uncovered 5 minutes. Stir in catsup and broth. Cover and cook until thickest pieces of chicken are done, about 20 minutes.

Remove chicken to warm platter; keep warm. Stir whipping cream into sauce in skillet. Mix cornstarch and water; gradually stir into sauce. Heat to boiling, stirring constantly. Boil and stir 1 minute. Pour sauce over chicken. Serve with hot cooked rice if desired.

Szechwan Chicken with Cashews

6 servings

2 large whole chicken breasts (about 2 pounds)
1 egg white
1 teaspoon cornstarch
1 teaspoon soy sauce
1 tablespoon cornstarch
1 tablespoon cold water
1 tablespoon soy sauce
3 tablespoons vegetable oil
1 medium onion, cut into 1-inch pieces
2 cloves garlic, finely chopped
1 large green pepper, cut into 1-inch pieces
1 can (8½ ounces) sliced bamboo shoots, drained
2 tablespoons chili sauce
1 teaspoon finely chopped dried chili pepper
1 tablespoon instant chicken bouillon
¼ cup water
¾ cup cashews

Remove bones and skin from chicken breasts; cut chicken into ¼-inch pieces. Mix egg white, 1 teaspoon cornstarch and 1 teaspoon soy sauce in glass or plastic bowl; stir in chicken. Cover and refrigerate 20 minutes.

Mix 1 tablespoon cornstarch, 1 tablespoon water and 1 tablespoon soy sauce. Heat oil in 12-inch skillet or wok over medium-high heat until hot. Cook and stir chicken in oil until chicken turns white; remove chicken from skillet with slotted spoon. Cook and stir onion and garlic in oil until garlic is light brown. Stir in chicken, green pepper, bamboo shoots, chili sauce and chili pepper; cook and stir 1 minute. Stir in instant bouillon and ¼ cup water. Heat to boiling. Stir in cornstarch mixture; cook and stir until thickened, about 30 seconds. Stir in cashews. Sprinkle with chopped green onions if desired.

Chicken & Mushrooms

4 servings

1   large whole chicken breast (about ¾ pound)
¼   cup all-purpose flour
¼   teaspoon salt
⅛   teaspoon pepper
2   tablespoons vegetable oil
1   can (7½ ounces) semi-condensed cream of
      mushroom soup
1   can (4 ounces) mushroom stems and pieces,
      drained
¼   cup dry white wine
2   cups hot cooked noodles

Remove bones and skin from chicken breast; cut into halves. Cut chicken into slices, 2 × ½ inch. Mix flour, salt and pepper. Coat chicken with flour mixture. Heat oil in 10-inch skillet over medium-high heat until hot. Cook and stir chicken in oil until brown, about 3 minutes. Stir in soup, mushrooms and wine. Heat to boiling; reduce heat. Cover and simmer until chicken is done, about 5 minutes. Serve over noodles.

Chicken Scallopini

4 servings

2   boneless chicken breasts
½   cup all-purpose flour
2   tablespoons vegetable oil
3   tablespoons margarine or butter
2   tablespoons lemon juice
      Snipped parsley
      Lemon slices
      Hot cooked spaghetti

Remove skin from chicken breasts; cut each into halves. Place each half between two pieces of waxed paper; pound until ¼ inch thick. Coat with flour. Heat oil and 2 tablespoons of the margarine in 12-inch skillet over medium heat until hot. Cook chicken until done and light brown, about 4 minutes on each side. Remove chicken to warm platter. Heat remaining margarine in same skillet until melted. Stir in lemon juice; pour over chicken. Garnish with snipped parsley and lemon slices. Serve with hot cooked spaghetti.

EASY STEPS FOR BONING A CHICKEN BREAST

With a good, sharp boning knife and a little practice, you can save money by boning your own chicken breast. Boned chicken breast can be cooked whole or cut into pieces for recipes.

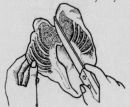

1. Turn chicken breast bone side up. Cut through the white gristle at neck end.

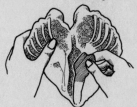

2. Bend breast back to pop keel bone (the wide center bone). Loosen keel bone and pull out.

3. Cut rib cages away from breast, cutting through shoulder joint.

4. Turn chicken breast over and cut away wishbone. Pull and remove tendons.

Sautéed Turkey
with Ham and Cheese

8 servings

2   tablespoons vegetable oil
2   tablespoons margarine or butter
1   pound uncooked boneless turkey breast,
        cut diagonally into ¼-inch slices
½   cup all-purpose flour
1   package (4 ounces) sliced fully cooked
        smoked ham, cut into halves
1   jar (2½ ounces) mushrooms, sliced, drained
        (reserve liquid)
¼   cup grated Parmesan cheese
¼   cup sweet white wine

Heat oil and margarine in 12-inch skillet until
hot. Coat turkey with flour. Cook turkey until
brown, about 4 minutes on each side. Arrange
in ungreased 12 × 7½ × 2-inch baking dish.
Top with ham slices; sprinkle with mushrooms
and cheese.

Pour reserved mushroom liquid into skillet.
Cook over medium heat, stirring occasionally,
30 seconds. Stir in wine; cook 30 seconds. Pour
over cheese. Cook uncovered in 400° oven
until cheese is melted, about 8 minutes.

Chicken and Noodles

6 servings

1   package (10 ounces) spinach noodles
1   cup milk
2   cans (6¾ ounces each) chunk chicken
1   can (4 ounces) mushroom stems and pieces,
        drained
1   small onion, finely chopped
¼   cup grated Romano cheese
2   tablespoons margarine or butter, melted
⅛   teaspoon pepper

Cook noodles as directed on package; drain.
Toss with remaining ingredients. Pour into
ungreased 2-quart casserole. Cover and cook
in 350° oven until hot, about 30 minutes. Stir
before serving. Serve with additional grated
Romano cheese if desired.

Sautéed Turkey with Ham and Cheese

One-Dish Chow Mein

5 servings

3 small stalks celery, sliced (about ¾ cup)
1 medium onion, chopped (about ½ cup)
1 tablespoon vegetable oil
2 cups cut-up cooked chicken or turkey
1 cup boiling water
½ cup uncooked regular rice
1 can (10¾ ounces) condensed cream of
     chicken soup
1 can (8 ounces) sliced water chestnuts, drained
1 can (4 ounces) mushroom stems and pieces,
     drained
1 jar (2 ounces) diced pimiento, drained
2 tablespoons soy sauce

Cook and stir celery and onion in oil in 3-quart saucepan over medium heat until onion is tender, about 5 minutes. Stir in remaining ingredients. Heat to boiling; reduce heat. Cover and simmer, stirring occasionally, until rice is tender, about 30 minutes. Sprinkle with chow mein noodles if desired.

EASY BROILED CHICKEN

Chickens weighing 2½ pounds or less are good for broiling. Cut whole chicken into halves or quarters. Turn wing tips onto back side. Place chicken, skin side down, on rack in broiler pan. Brush chicken with melted margarine or butter. Place broil pan so top of chicken is 7 to 9 inches from heat. (If broiler pan cannot be placed that far from heat, reduce oven temperature to 450°.)

Broil chicken 30 minutes. Sprinkle brown side with salt and pepper if desired. Turn chicken; brush with melted margarine. Broil until chicken is crisp and brown and thickest pieces are done, 20 to 30 minutes longer.

Chicken Liver Stroganoff

6 servings

2 tablespoons margarine or butter
2 tablespoons vegetable oil
1 medium onion, chopped (about ½ cup)
1 can (4 ounces) mushroom stems and pieces,
     drained (reserve liquid)
1 pound chicken livers, cut into halves
½ cup water
2 tablespoons all-purpose flour
2 tablespoons catsup
½ teaspoon salt
¼ teaspoon garlic powder
1 cup dairy sour cream

Heat margarine and oil in 10-inch skillet until hot. Add onion and mushrooms. Cook and stir until onion is tender, about 5 minutes; remove from skillet. Stir in chicken livers. Cook, stirring occasionally, until light brown, about 4 minutes. Shake reserved mushroom liquid, the water, flour, catsup, salt and garlic powder in tightly covered container; gradually stir into chicken livers. Heat to boiling; reduce heat. Cover and simmer 5 minutes. Stir in onion and mushrooms; remove from heat. Stir in sour cream. Serve over hot cooked rice or noodles if desired.

Chicken Livers with Pasta

4 servings

1 package (7 ounces) bite-size spaghetti
½ pound chicken livers, cut into 1-inch pieces
1 can (4 ounces) mushroom stems and pieces,
     drained
1 tablespoon vegetable oil
2 tablespoons margarine or butter
¼ cup whipping cream
2 tablespoons grated Parmesan cheese
1 jar (2 ounces) diced pimiento, drained

Cook spaghetti as directed on package; drain. Cook livers and mushrooms in oil, stirring occasionally, until livers are brown, about 8 minutes. Toss spaghetti with margarine, cream and cheese. Stir in livers and pimiento.

Marinated Chicken

8 servings

2½ - to 3-pound broiler-fryer chicken, cut up
¼   cup vegetable oil
¼   cup lemon juice
¼   cup dry white wine
2   teaspoons dried oregano leaves
2   cloves garlic, finely chopped

Cut each chicken breast half into halves. Arrange chicken in ungreased 13 × 9 × 2-inch baking dish. Mix remaining ingredients; pour over chicken. Cover and refrigerate at least 1 hour but no longer than 24 hours.

TO SERVE: About 65 minutes before serving, remove chicken from marinade; reserve marinade. Place chicken, skin sides down, on rack in broiler pan. Set oven control to broil and/or 550°. Broil chicken with top 7 to 9 inches from heat 30 minutes. Turn chicken; brush with marinade. Broil until brown and crisp and thickest pieces are done, 20 to 30 minutes longer.

Chicken-Rice Casserole

8 servings

2½ - to 3-pound broiler-fryer chicken, cut up
⅓   cup all-purpose flour
1   teaspoon salt
1   teaspoon lemon pepper
2   tablespoons margarine or butter
1   clove garlic, finely chopped
1   cup uncooked regular rice
1   package (10 ounces) frozen carrots and peas
1   can (10¾ ounces) condensed chicken broth
1   cup water
1   teaspoon dried basil leaves
½   teaspoon dried marjoram leaves

Cut each chicken breast half into halves. Mix flour, salt and lemon pepper. Coat chicken with flour mixture. Heat margarine and garlic in 12-inch skillet until margarine is melted. Cook chicken in margarine over medium heat until light brown, about 15 minutes; remove chicken. Cook and stir rice in same skillet until brown, about 4 minutes. Rinse frozen carrots and peas under running cold water to separate; drain. Mix rice, carrots and peas, broth, water, basil and marjoram in ungreased 3-quart casserole. Arrange chicken on rice mixture. (To serve immediately, continue as directed in TO SERVE except — decrease cook time to about 1 hour.) Cover and refrigerate no longer than 24 hours.

TO SERVE: About 1 hour 20 minutes before serving, cook Chicken-Rice Casserole covered in 375° oven until rice is done, about 1¼ hours.

Chicken in Wine Sauce

8 servings

6   slices bacon
2½ - to 3-pound broiler-fryer chicken, cut up
2½ cups dry red wine
1   can (10¾ ounces) condensed chicken broth
1   tablespoon catsup
½   teaspoon dried thyme leaves
½   teaspoon salt
¼   teaspoon pepper
2   cloves garlic, finely chopped
½   cup cold water
¼   cup all-purpose flour
1   jar (16 ounces) whole onions, drained
1   can (4 ounces) mushroom stems and pieces, drained

Fry bacon in 4-quart Dutch oven until crisp; drain and crumble. Cook chicken in fat over medium heat until light brown, about 5 minutes on each side. Stir in bacon, wine, broth, catsup, thyme, salt, pepper and garlic. Heat to boiling; reduce heat. Cover and simmer until chicken is done, 40 to 45 minutes.

Remove chicken; skim fat. Shake water and flour in tightly covered container; gradually stir into broth. Heat to boiling, stirring constantly. Boil and stir 1 minute. Stir in onions and mushrooms; return chicken to sauce. (To serve immediately, boil 2 minutes.) Cover and refrigerate no longer than 48 hours.

TO SERVE: About 25 minutes before serving, heat Chicken in Wine Sauce to boiling; reduce heat. Cover and simmer until chicken is hot, 15 to 18 minutes.

Oven-Fried Chicken

3 meals - 8 servings each

3 2½- to 3-pound broiler-fryer chickens, cut up
1½ cups all-purpose flour
1 tablespoon paprika
2½ teaspoons salt
¾ teaspoon pepper
½ cup margarine or butter
½ cup shortening

Cut each chicken breast half into halves. Mix flour, paprika, salt and pepper. Coat chicken with flour mixture. Heat half each of the margarine and shortening in each of two 15½ × 10½ × 1-inch jelly roll pans in 425° oven until melted. Place chicken, skin sides down, in pans. Stagger pans on oven racks. Cook uncovered 30 minutes. Turn chicken; rotate pans. Cook uncovered until thickest pieces of chicken are done, about 30 minutes longer. (To serve immediately, remove 10 pieces of chicken and serve.) Refrigerate until cool. Divide chicken into 3 portions. Wrap each portion in heavy-duty aluminum foil. Label and freeze no longer than 1 month.

TO SERVE: About 45 minutes before serving, remove 1 package Oven-Fried Chicken from freezer. Open foil and place on oven rack. Heat in 400° oven 20 minutes. Separate into single layer; heat until hot and crisp, about 20 minutes longer.

Crunchy Chicken Salad

4 servings

¾ cup mayonnaise or salad dressing
1 tablespoon sugar
1 teaspoon grated lemon peel
1 tablespoon lemon juice
½ teaspoon ground ginger
¼ teaspoon salt
2 cups cut-up cooked chicken or turkey
1 cup seedless green or red grapes
2 medium stalks celery, sliced (about 1 cup)
¼ cup sliced almonds
1 tablespoon plus 1 teaspoon sugar

Have ready at serving time:

Lettuce leaves

Mix mayonnaise, 1 tablespoon sugar, the lemon peel and lemon juice, ginger and salt. Stir in chicken, grapes and celery. Cover and refrigerate at least 4 hours but no longer than 24 hours.

Cook almonds and 1 tablespoon plus 1 teaspoon sugar over low heat, stirring constantly, until sugar is melted and almonds are coated. Cool; break apart. Store at room temperature.

TO SERVE: At serving time, spoon Crunchy Chicken Salad into lettuce-lined bowl. Sprinkle with almonds.

Oven-Fried Chicken

Italian-Style Chicken

2 meals - 6 servings each

6 small whole chicken breasts (about 4 pounds)
1 cup dry bread crumbs
1/2 cup finely chopped walnuts
1 teaspoon salt
3 eggs
1/4 cup water
3/4 cup all-purpose flour
1/4 cup margarine or butter
1/4 cup vegetable oil
1 can (10 3/4 ounces) condensed chicken broth
1 1/2 cups shredded mozzarella cheese
        (about 6 ounces)
1 can (8 ounces) mushroom stems and pieces,
        drained and coarsely chopped
1 cup chili sauce
1/2 cup dry white wine
1 teaspoon dried marjoram leaves

Remove bones and skin from chicken breasts; cut each into halves. Mix bread crumbs, walnuts and salt. Beat eggs slightly; stir in water. Coat chicken breasts with flour; dip into egg mixture. Coat with crumb mixture. Heat margarine and oil in 10-inch skillet over medium heat until hot. Cook chicken, several pieces at a time, until golden brown, 2 to 3 minutes. Place 6 chicken breast halves in each of 2 ungreased 12 × 7 1/2 × 1-inch baking dishes or 9 × 9 × 2-inch baking pans. Pour broth into dishes; sprinkle with cheese. Mix remaining ingredients; spoon over top. (To serve 1 dish immediately, cook uncovered in 375° oven until chicken is done, about 30 minutes.) Wrap, label and freeze no longer than 1 month.

TO SERVE: About 1 1/4 hours before serving, remove 1 dish Italian-Style Chicken from freezer and unwrap. Cover and cook in 375° oven until hot, about 40 minutes. Uncover and cook until done, about 30 minutes longer.

Chicken Mozzarella

8 servings

2 large whole chicken breasts (about 1 1/2 pounds)
1 cup finely shredded mozzarella cheese
1/2 teaspoon fennel seed
1/4 teaspoon salt
1 clove garlic, crushed
1/2 cup all-purpose flour
2 eggs, well beaten
1/2 cup dry bread crumbs

Have ready at serving time:

Vegetable oil

Remove bones and skin from chicken breasts; cut each into halves. Place each half between 2 pieces of waxed paper; pound until 1/4 inch thick (be careful not to tear meat). Mix cheese, fennel seed, salt and garlic. Spoon 1/4 of the cheese mixture onto center of each chicken breast. Fold chicken over cheese (make sure cheese is completely enclosed). Secure with wooden picks. Roll chicken in flour, then dip into egg; coat completely with bread crumbs. Repeat. Shape chicken into ovals. (To serve immediately, cover and refrigerate at least 1 hour. Heat oil [1 1/2 to 2 inches] in deep-fat fryer or Dutch oven to 360°. Fry until deep golden brown, about 8 minutes. Drain on paper towels. Cut each piece into halves. Serve with lemon wedges if desired.) Wrap, label and freeze no longer than 1 month.

TO SERVE: About 24 hours before serving, remove Chicken Mozzarella from freezer. Refrigerate wrapped chicken until thawed, at least 24 hours. Heat oil (1 1/2 to 2 inches) in deep-fat fryer or Dutch oven to 360°. Fry until deep golden brown, about 11 minutes. Drain on paper towels. Cut each piece into halves. Serve with lemon wedges if desired.

Chicken-Vegetable Pie

2 meals - 6 servings each

8 slices bacon, cut up
1 large onion, coarsely chopped (about 1 cup)
2 medium stalks celery, sliced (about 1 cup)
2 medium carrots, coarsely chopped (about 1 cup)
2 envelopes (about .87 ounce each) chicken gravy mix
2 envelopes (about 1 ounce each) hollandaise sauce mix
3 cups cold water
4 cups cut-up cooked chicken or turkey
1 can (12 ounces) whole kernel corn with peppers, drained
½ teaspoon poultry seasoning
   Pastry (below)

Fry bacon in 4-quart Dutch oven until crisp; remove bacon with slotted spoon. Drain on paper towels; reserve. Drain fat, reserving 2 tablespoons in pan. Cook and stir onion, celery and carrots in fat until carrots are crisp-tender, about 5 minutes. Stir in gravy mixes and sauce mixes; gradually stir in water. Heat to boiling; reduce heat. Stir in chicken, corn, poultry seasoning and reserved bacon. Simmer uncovered 5 minutes. Divide mixture between 2 ungreased 8 × 8 × 2-inch baking pans.

Prepare Pastry; divide into halves. Shape 1 half into flattened round on lightly floured cloth-covered board. Roll into 9-inch square with floured stockinet-covered rolling pin; place over mixture in pan. Roll edges under; flute. Cut slits in center to allow steam to escape. Repeat with remaining pastry. (To serve 1 pan immediately, bake in 425° oven until crust is brown, 35 to 40 minutes. Let stand 10 minutes before cutting.) Freeze uncovered just until crust is firm, about 1 hour. Wrap, label and freeze no longer than 3 months.

Pastry

⅔ cup plus 2 tablespoons shortening
2 cups all-purpose flour
1 teaspoon salt
4 to 5 tablespoons cold water

Cut shortening into flour and salt until particles are size of small peas. Sprinkle in water, 1 tablespoon at a time, tossing with fork until all flour is moistened and pastry almost cleans side of bowl (1 to 2 teaspoons water can be added if necessary.)

TO SERVE: About 1½ hours before serving, remove 1 pan Chicken-Vegetable Pie from freezer and unwrap. Cover edges loosely with 2- to 3-inch strip of aluminum foil to prevent excessive browning. Bake in 450° oven until crust is brown and mixture is hot, about 1¼ hours. Let stand 10 minutes before cutting.

Freezer Chicken Mix

3 meals - 4 to 8 servings each

3 2½- to 3-pound broiler-fryer chickens, cut up
3 parsley sprigs
2 stalks celery (with leaves), cut up
2 carrots, cut up
1 medium onion, sliced
2 teaspoons seasoned salt
½ teaspoon pepper
1¾ cups cold water
1 cup all-purpose flour
2 teaspoons salt
½ teaspoon pepper

Place chicken and giblets in 6-quart Dutch oven. Add just enough water to cover. Add parsley, celery, carrots, onion, seasoned salt and ½ teaspoon pepper. Heat to boiling; reduce heat. Cover and simmer until chicken is done, about 45 minutes. Remove chicken from broth; refrigerate until cool.

Remove chicken from bones and skin; cut into pieces. Cover and refrigerate while preparing gravy. Strain broth; pour 6 cups into 3-quart saucepan. Shake water, flour, salt and pepper in tightly covered container; gradually stir into broth. Heat to boiling, stirring constantly. Boil and stir 1 minute. Divide cooked chicken (about 2 cups each) among three 1-quart freezer containers. Pour 2 cups gravy over each. Cover, label and freeze no longer than 4 months. Use Freezer Chicken Mix in Chicken Chowder (page 51), Chicken a la King (page 51) or Chicken-Broccoli Deluxe (page 51).

Chicken Chowder

8 servings

1   container Freezer Chicken Mix (page 50)
1   package (6 ounces) hash brown potato mix
      with onions
1   can (12 ounces) whole kernel corn with
      peppers
6   cups milk
1   tablespoon snipped parsley
1½ teaspoons seasoned salt
½   teaspoon paprika
4   slices bacon, crisply fried and crumbled,
      or ¼ cup imitation bacon

Dip container of Freezer Chicken Mix into very hot water just to loosen. Heat frozen block in 4-quart Dutch oven over medium heat, stirring occasionally, until thawed, about 30 minutes. Stir in potatoes, corn (with liquid), milk, parsley, seasoned salt and paprika. Heat over medium heat, stirring occasionally, until potatoes are tender, 15 to 20 minutes. Sprinkle with bacon.

Chicken a la King

4 servings

1   container Freezer Chicken Mix (page 50)
1   can (4 ounces) mushroom stems and pieces
1   jar (2 ounces) diced pimiento
1   small green pepper, chopped (about ½ cup)
¼   cup dry white wine
      Patty shells or hot cooked rice
¼   cup toasted slivered almonds

Dip container of Freezer Chicken Mix into very hot water just to loosen. Heat frozen block in 3-quart saucepan over medium heat, stirring occasionally, until thawed, about 30 minutes. Stir in mushrooms (with liquid), pimiento (with liquid) and green pepper. Heat to boiling; reduce heat. Cover and simmer, stirring occasionally, until chicken is hot and green pepper is crisp-tender, 8 to 10 minutes. Stir in wine. Serve over patty shells. Sprinkle with almonds.

Chicken-Broccoli Deluxe

6 servings

1   container Freezer Chicken Mix (page 50)
1   cup dairy sour cream
½   cup sliced pitted ripe olives
½   teaspoon ground nutmeg
2   packages (10 ounces each) frozen broccoli
      spears or asparagus spears
½   cup grated Parmesan cheese

Dip container of Freezer Chicken Mix into very hot water just to loosen. Heat frozen block in 3-quart saucepan over medium heat, stirring occasionally, until thawed, about 30 minutes. Heat to boiling; reduce heat. Stir in sour cream, olives and nutmeg; heat just until hot.

Cook broccoli as directed on package; drain. Arrange broccoli in ungreased 12 × 7½ × 2-inch baking dish or heatproof platter. Pour chicken mixture over broccoli; sprinkle with cheese. Set oven control to broil and/or 550°. Broil with top 3 to 5 inches from heat until cheese is light brown, about 5 minutes.

Microwave Directions: Dip container of Freezer Chicken Mix into very hot water just to loosen. Place frozen block in 3-quart microwaveproof casserole. Cover tightly and microwave on high (100%), stirring every 3 minutes, until thawed, 9 to 11 minutes; stir. Cover and microwave 5 minutes longer. Stir in sour cream, olives and nutmeg. Cover and microwave until hot, 3 to 5 minutes. Continue as directed except — arrange broccoli in microwaveproof dish or platter. Cover and microwave 3 minutes; rotate dish ¼ turn. Microwave until hot, 2 to 3 minutes longer.

Fish with Vegetables

5 servings

1   *pound fish fillets*
1/2 *teaspoon salt*
1/8 *teaspoon pepper*
2   *tablespoons margarine or butter, melted*
1   *tablespoon lemon juice*
1   *medium zucchini, cut into 1/4-inch slices*
1   *small green pepper, cut into 1/4-inch strips*
1   *small red onion, sliced*
2   *tablespoons margarine or butter*

If fish fillets are large, cut into 5 serving pieces. Arrange fish in ungreased $12 \times 7\frac{1}{2} \times 2$- or $8 \times 8 \times 2$-inch baking dish; sprinkle with salt and pepper. Mix 2 tablespoons margarine and the lemon juice; pour over fish. Cook uncovered in 350° oven until fish flakes easily with fork, 20 to 25 minutes.

Cook zucchini, green pepper and onion in 2 tablespoons margarine over medium heat, stirring occasionally, until crisp-tender, 5 to 7 minutes. Serve vegetables over fish.

Crunchy Oven-Fried Fish

5 servings

1   *pound fish fillets*
1/3 *cup dairy sour cream*
1   *tablespoon lemon juice*
1/2 *teaspoon chili powder*
3/4 *cup finely crushed corn chips*
2   *tablespoons margarine or butter, melted*

If fish fillets are large, cut into 5 serving pieces. Mix sour cream, lemon juice and chili powder. Dip fish into sour cream mixture; coat with chips. Place in generously greased $13 \times 9 \times 2$-inch baking dish. Pour margarine over fish. Place dish on oven rack that is slightly above middle position of oven. Cook uncovered in 500° oven until fish flakes easily with fork, 10 to 12 minutes. Serve with sliced avocado and tomatoes if desired.

Fish with Peppers

5 servings

1   *pound fish fillets*
3   *tablespoons soy sauce*
1   *clove garlic, finely chopped*
1/4 *teaspoon ground ginger*
2   *medium green peppers, cut into 1-inch pieces*
8   *ounces mushrooms, cut into halves*
3   *tablespoons vegetable oil*

If fish fillets are large, cut into 5 serving pieces. Mix soy sauce, garlic and ginger; brush on both sides of fish. Cook and stir green peppers and mushrooms in oil in 10-inch skillet over medium-high heat until crisp-tender, about 6 minutes. Remove vegetables with slotted spoon; reserve. Fry fish in same skillet until fish flakes easily with fork, about 8 minutes. Add vegetables; heat just until hot. Serve with hot cooked rice if desired.

Fish Divan

5 servings

1   *package (16 ounces) frozen fish fillets*
2   *packages (10 ounces each) frozen broccoli spears*
1   *teaspoon salt*
1   *can (10¾ ounces) condensed cream of chicken soup*
1/2 *cup milk*
1   *can (3 ounces) French fried onions*

Cut frozen fish crosswise into 5 equal parts (let stand at room temperature 10 minutes before cutting). Rinse frozen broccoli under running cold water to separate; drain. (If broccoli stems are more than 1/2 inch in diameter, cut lengthwise into halves.) Place fish in center of ungreased $13 \times 9 \times 2$-inch baking dish. Arrange broccoli around fish. Sprinkle fish and broccoli with salt. Mix soup and milk; pour over top. Cook uncovered in 350° oven until fish flakes easily with fork, about 30 minutes. Sprinkle with onions; cook 5 minutes longer.

Fish with Vegetables, and Crunchy Oven-Fried Fish

Fish Piquant

5 servings

1   *package (16 ounces) frozen fish fillets*
1/2   *teaspoon salt*
1/2   *cup tartar sauce*
1   *can (3 ounces) French fried onions*

Cut frozen fish crosswise into 5 equal parts (let stand at room temperature 10 minutes before cutting). Arrange fish in ungreased 8 × 8 × 2- or 12 × 7½ × 2-inch baking dish; sprinkle with salt. Cook uncovered in 450° oven until fish flakes easily with fork, 25 to 30 minutes. Spread tartar sauce on fish; top with onions. Cook until sauce is hot and onions are crisp, 3 to 5 minutes.

Hot Mexican-Style Fish

5 servings

1   *package (16 ounces) frozen skinless halibut*
   or haddock fillets
2   *tablespoons margarine or butter, melted*
1/2   *teaspoon salt*
1   *jar (8 ounces) jalapeño salsa*
1   *can (2.2 ounces) sliced ripe olives, drained*

Place frozen block of fish on 20 × 12-inch piece of heavy-duty aluminum foil; seal securely. Cook on ungreased cookie sheet in 450° oven 25 minutes. Turn back foil; pour margarine over fish. Sprinkle wtih salt; top with salsa and olives. Cook uncovered until sauce is hot, about 10 minutes. Serve with lemon or lime wedges if desired.

Saucy Fish

8 servings

Prepare 1 package (24 ounces) batter-fried fillets or 2 packages (14 ounces each) frozen fish sticks as directed on package. Serve with one of the following sauces.

Almond Sauce

1/2   *cup sliced almonds*
1   *tablespoon margarine or butter*
1   *can (10¾ ounces) condensed cream of*
   chicken soup
1   *cup milk*
2   *tablespoons snipped parsley*

Cook and stir almonds in margarine in 1-quart saucepan until light brown; remove almonds with slotted spoon and reserve. Heat remaining ingredients in same pan, stirring occasionally, until hot. Pour over fish; sprinkle with reserved almonds.

Creamed Pea Sauce

1   *package (8 ounces) frozen peas with*
   cream sauce
1   *cup milk*
1/8   *teaspoon dried dill weed*
1   *teaspoon prepared mustard*

Heat all ingredients to boiling in 2-quart saucepan over medium heat, stirring occasionally; reduce heat. Cover and simmer 1 minute. Remove from heat; stir.

Chili Sauce

1   *small onion, chopped (about ¼ cup)*
2   *tablespoons margarine or butter*
1/2   *cup chili sauce*
1/4   *cup orange marmalade*
1/4   *teaspoon salt*

Cook and stir onion in margarine in 1-quart saucepan until tender. Stir in remaining ingredients. Heat, stirring occasionally, until hot.

Fish and Sweet Potatoes

4 servings

1 package (15 ounces) batter-fried fish fillets
1 can (18 ounces) vacuum pack sweet potatoes
½ cup apricot preserves
2 tablespoons catsup
2 tablespoons lemon juice
2 green onions (with tops), sliced

Place fish in ungreased 13 × 9 × 2-inch baking dish. Cook uncovered in 425° oven 20 minutes. Arrange sweet potatoes around fish. Mix preserves, catsup and lemon juice; brush on fish and potatoes. Cook uncovered until potatoes are hot, about 10 minutes. Sprinkle with green onions.

Tuna Spaghetti

5 servings

1 package (7 ounces) thin spaghetti
2 cloves garlic, finely chopped
¼ cup margarine or butter
¾ cup half-and-half
1 teaspoon dried basil leaves
¼ teaspoon dried oregano leaves
1 can (9¼ ounces) tuna, drained
½ cup sliced pimiento-stuffed olives
¼ cup grated Parmesan cheese

Cook spaghetti as directed on package; drain. Cook garlic in margarine in 2-quart saucepan until golden brown. Stir in half-and-half, basil and oregano. Heat to boiling. Stir in tuna, olives and cheese; boil and stir 1 minute. Pour over hot spaghetti. Sprinkle with snipped parsley if desired.

Tuna-Macaroni Skillet

Tuna-Macaroni Skillet

6 servings

1 can (10¾ ounces) condensed cream of
   chicken soup
2¼ cups water
1 package (10 ounces) frozen mixed vegetables
1 package (7 ounces) elbow macaroni
¼ teaspoon dried dill weed
2 cans (6½ ounces each) tuna, drained
1 can (3 ounces) French fried onions

Mix soup and water in 10-inch skillet; stir in vegetables, macaroni and dill weed. Heat to boiling, stirring occasionally; reduce heat. Cover and simmer, stirring occasionally, until macaroni is tender, about 15 minutes. Stir in tuna; heat until hot, about 3 minutes. Sprinkle with onions.

Shrimp and Zucchini

4 servings

1 can (8¼ ounces) pineapple chunks, drained
   (reserve syrup)
1 package (12 ounces) frozen uncooked, peeled
   and deveined medium shrimp
1 tablespoon cornstarch
2 tablespoons cold water
3 tablespoons vegetable oil
1 clove garlic, finely chopped
1 medium onion, sliced
1 medium zucchini, cut into ¼-inch slices
1 tablespoon soy sauce
1 teaspoon sugar
¼ teaspoon ground ginger
2 medium tomatoes, cut into wedges

Add enough water to reserved pineapple
syrup to measure ½ cup. Rinse frozen shrimp
under running cold water to separate; drain.
Mix cornstarch and water. Heat oil in 10-inch
skillet over medium-high heat until hot. Cook
and stir shrimp, garlic, onion and zucchini in
oil until vegetables are crisp-tender, about 3
minutes. Add reserved pineapple syrup, the
soy sauce, sugar and ginger. Heat to boiling;
stir in cornstarch mixture. Cook and stir until
thickened, about 10 seconds. Stir in pineapple
and tomatoes; heat just until hot. Serve with
hot cooked rice if desired.

Shrimp-Rice Salad

6 servings

1 package (6 ounces) frozen Chinese pea pods
3 cups cooked rice
2 cans (4¼ ounces each) medium shrimp,
   rinsed and drained
2 medium stalks celery, diagonally sliced
   (about 1 cup)
½ cup mayonnaise or salad dressing
¼ cup chopped green onions (with tops)
¼ teaspoon ground ginger
¼ teaspoon ground cinnamon

Have ready at serving time:

1 can (11 ounces) mandarin orange segments,
   drained
  Salad greens
¾ cup salted cashews or peanuts

Rinse frozen pea pods under running cold
water to separate; drain. Mix pea pods, rice,
shrimp, celery, mayonnaise, onions, ginger
and cinnamon. Cover and refrigerate at least 2
hours but no longer than 24 hours.

TO SERVE: At serving time, toss orange segments with shrimp mixture. Spoon onto salad
greens; sprinkle with cashews.

Shrimp and Zucchini

Baked Coconut Fish

5 servings

1 pound fish fillets
1 teaspoon salt
1 small onion, sliced and separated into rings
½ cup milk
½ cup flaked coconut
1 teaspoon grated lime peel
2 tablespoons lime juice
¼ teaspoon garlic powder

Have ready at serving time:

½ cup flaked coconut
2 tablespoons margarine or butter, melted

If fish fillets are large, cut into 5 serving pieces. Place fish in shallow glass or plastic dish; sprinkle with salt. Arrange onion on fish. Mix milk, ½ cup coconut, the lime peel, lime juice and garlic powder; pour over onion and fish. Cover and refrigerate at least 8 hours but no longer than 24 hours.

TO SERVE: About 40 minutes before serving, remove fish and onion from marinade. Place onion in ungreased 8 × 8 × 2-inch baking dish; top with fish. Place ½ cup coconut on fish; pour margarine over top. Cover and cook in 375° oven 15 minutes. Uncover and cook until golden brown and fish flakes easily with fork, about 15 minutes longer. Garnish with lime wedges or slices if desired.

Broiled Marinated Cod

6 servings

1 pound cod fillets
1 teaspoon grated lemon peel
3 tablespoons lemon juice
2 tablespoons soy sauce
1 tablespoon vegetable oil
2 teaspoons sugar
½ teaspoon ground ginger
¼ teaspoon garlic powder

If fish fillets are large, cut into 6 serving pieces; place in shallow glass or plastic dish. Mix remaining ingredients; brush on both sides of fish. Cover and refrigerate at least 8 hours but no longer than 24 hours.

TO SERVE: About 15 minutes before serving, place fish on rack in broiler pan. Set oven control to broil and/or 550°. Broil fish with tops 2 to 3 inches from heat until light brown, about 5 minutes. Brush with marinade; turn carefully. Broil, brushing occasionally with marinade, until fish flakes easily with fork, 5 to 8 minutes longer. Garnish with snipped parsley and lemon wedges if desired.

Impossible Salmon Pie

Impossible Salmon Pie

6 servings

1   can (15½ ounces) salmon, drained
1   medium onion, chopped (about ½ cup)
1   small green pepper, chopped (about ½ cup)
½   cup shredded Swiss cheese
1½   cups milk
¾   cup buttermilk baking mix
3   eggs
½   teaspoon dried tarragon leaves
½   teaspoon salt
⅛   teaspoon pepper

Sprinkle salmon, onion, green pepper and cheese evenly in lightly greased 10 × 1½-inch pie plate. Beat remaining ingredients until smooth, 15 seconds in blender on high speed or 1 minute with hand beater. Pour evenly into pie plate. (To serve immediately, continue as directed in TO SERVE except — decrease baking time to about 30 minutes.) Cover and refrigerate no longer than 24 hours.

TO SERVE: About 40 minutes before serving, cook Impossible Salmon Pie uncovered in 400° oven until knife inserted in center comes out clean, about 35 minutes.

Marinated Tarragon Salmon

4 servings

3   slices lemon
1   teaspoon salt
¼   teaspoon dried dill weed
2   salmon steaks (about 1 inch thick)
1   small onion, thinly sliced
¼   cup wine vinegar
¼   teaspoon dried tarragon leaves

Have ready at serving time:

1   small cucumber
½   cup plain yogurt
¼   teaspoon salt
⅛   teaspoon dried dill weed
     Lettuce leaves
2   medium tomatoes, sliced

Heat 1 inch water, the lemon, 1 teaspoon salt and ¼ teaspoon dill weed to boiling in 10-inch skillet; reduce heat. Arrange salmon in skillet. Simmer uncovered until salmon flakes easily with fork, 6 to 8 minutes; drain. Carefully remove skin from salmon. Place salmon in shallow glass or plastic dish; arrange onion on fish. Mix vinegar and tarragon; drizzle over onion and fish. Cover and refrigerate at least 8 hours but no longer than 24 hours.

TO SERVE: About 20 minutes before serving, cut cucumber lengthwise into halves; remove seeds. Cut both halves crosswise into thin slices. Mix cucumber, yogurt, ¼ teaspoon salt and ⅛ teaspoon dill weed. Place salmon on lettuce leaves; arrange onion and tomatoes around fish. Drizzle any remaining marinade over fish. Serve with cucumber mixture. Garnish with fresh dill or watercress if desired.

EASY MARINATED TARRAGON SALMON: Substitute 1 can (15½ ounces) salmon, drained, for the salmon steaks; do not cook. Carefully separate salmon just enough to remove bones and skin. Top with onion and tarragon; pour vinegar over top. Cover and refrigerate at least 1 hour but no longer than 24 hours. Continue as directed in TO SERVE.

Tuna Mousse

6 servings

2   envelopes (1 tablespoon each) unflavored
      gelatin
1/4   cup cold water
1/2   cup boiling water
1   package (8 ounces) cream cheese, softened
2   tablespoons lemon juice
1/2   teaspoon salt
2   medium stalks celery, chopped (about 1 cup)
1   small green pepper, chopped (about 1/2 cup)
1   can (9 1/4 ounces) tuna, drained
1   cup whipping cream

Have ready at serving time:

   Salad greens
3   *hard-cooked eggs, cut into fourths*
   Cherry tomatoes
   Lemon wedges

Sprinkle gelatin on cold water in 2-quart bowl
to soften; gradually stir in boiling water. Stir in
cream cheese, lemon juice and salt until cheese
is melted and mixture is smooth. Stir in celery,
green pepper and tuna. Beat whipping cream
in chilled 2-quart bowl until stiff; fold in tuna
mixture. Pour into ungreased 9 × 5 × 3-inch
loaf pan or 7-cup mold. Refrigerate until firm,
at least 1 hour but no longer than 48 hours.

TO SERVE: At serving time, unmold Tuna
Mousse on salad greens. Arrange eggs, tomatoes and lemon wedges around mousse.

Tuna Linguine Casserole

6 servings

16   ounces uncooked linguine or spaghetti
2   cans (10 3/4 ounces each) condensed cream
      of mushroom soup
2   cans (10 3/4 ounces each) condensed cream
      of chicken soup
1 1/2   cups milk
1/4   cup dry white wine
2   cans (4 ounces each) mushroom stems and
      pieces, drained
2   cans (9 1/4 ounces each) tuna, drained
1   cup grated Parmesan cheese

Cook linguine as directed on package; drain.
Mix 1 can mushroom soup, 1 can chicken
soup, 3/4 cup milk and 2 tablespoons wine in
ungreased 8 × 8 × 2-inch baking pan. Stir in
half of the linguine, 1 can mushrooms and 1
can tuna. Sprinkle with 1/2 cup of the cheese.
Repeat with remaining ingredients. (To serve
1 pan immediately, cook uncovered in 375°
oven until hot and bubbly, about 30 minutes.) Wrap, label and freeze no longer than
2 months.

TO SERVE: About 1 1/2 hours before serving,
remove 1 pan Tuna Linguine Casserole from
freezer and unwrap. Cook uncovered in 425°
oven until hot and bubbly, 80 to 90 minutes.

Cheese, Eggs & Dried Beans

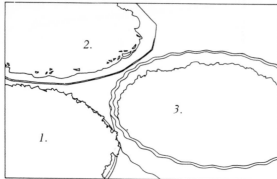

1. Vegetable Bean Salad, 2. Broccoli-Mushroom Spaghetti,
3. Scrambled Egg Pie

Fettuccine with Pepperoni

6 servings

1 package (16 ounces) fettuccine noodles
1 package (about 4 ounces) sliced pepperoni
1 can (8 ounces) mushroom stems and pieces,
     drained
2 tablespoons margarine or butter
3/4 cup half-and-half
1/2 cup grated Parmesan cheese
1 tablespoon snipped parsley, if desired

Cook fettuccine as directed on package; drain.
Cut pepperoni slices into halves. Cook pepperoni in 2-quart saucepan over medium heat
until light brown; drain and reserve. Cook
mushrooms in margarine in same pan, stirring occasionally, until mushrooms are light
brown. Stir in half-and-half and cheese; heat
just until hot. Stir in reserved pepperoni and
the parsley; toss with fettuccine. Serve with
additional grated Parmesan cheese if desired.

Cheese Ravioli

6 servings

1 package (30 ounces) frozen cheese-filled
     ravioli
1 can (11 ounces) condensed Cheddar cheese
     soup
1 1/4 cups milk
1 cup shredded mozzarella cheese
     (about 4 ounces)
1/2 teaspoon Italian seasoning
1/2 cup grated Parmesan cheese

Cook ravioli as directed on package; drain.
Place ravioli in ungreased 2-quart casserole or
heatproof serving dish. Heat soup and milk
just to boiling in 2-quart saucepan, stirring
occasionally. Stir in mozzarella cheese and
Italian seasoning. Cook over low heat, stirring
constantly, until cheese is melted. Pour cheese
mixture over ravioli; sprinkle with Parmesan
cheese. Set oven control to broil and/or 550°.
Broil ravioli with top 3 to 4 inches from heat
until cheese is light brown, 3 to 4 minutes.

Chili-Cheese Macaroni Casserole

5 servings

1 package (7 ounces) elbow macaroni
1 can (4 ounces) chopped green chilies, drained
2 cups shredded Cheddar cheese (about 8 ounces)
1 cup dairy sour cream
1/4 cup finely chopped onion
1/2 teaspoon salt
1/2 teaspoon dried oregano leaves
6 slices bacon, crisply fried and crumbled
1 cup seasoned croutons

Cook macaroni as directed on package; drain.
Mix macaroni, chilies, 1 1/2 cups of the cheese,
the sour cream, onion, salt and oregano in
ungreased 2-quart casserole. Mix bacon,
croutons and the remaining cheese; sprinkle
over macaroni. Cook uncovered in 375° oven
until hot and bubbly, 25 to 30 minutes.

Spaghetti-Cheese Toss

6 servings

1   package (16 ounces) thin spaghetti
8   slices bacon, cut up
½   cup dry white wine
3   eggs, well beaten
½   cup grated Parmesan cheese
2   tablespoons snipped parsley
    Freshly ground pepper

Cook spaghetti in 4-quart Dutch oven as directed on package; drain. Return to pan. Fry bacon over medium heat until crisp; remove bacon with slotted spoon and drain on paper towels. Stir wine into fat; heat to boiling. Toss wine mixture and bacon with spaghetti. Add eggs, cheese and parsley; toss over low heat until egg adheres to spaghetti and appears cooked. Serve with freshly ground pepper and, if desired, additional grated Parmesan cheese.

Broccoli-Mushroom Spaghetti

5 servings

1   package (10 ounces) frozen chopped broccoli
1   jar (4½ ounces) sliced mushrooms, drained
¼   cup margarine or butter
½   teaspoon salt
⅛   teaspoon pepper
1   package (7 ounces) spaghetti
½   cup grated Parmesan cheese
1   tablespoon lemon juice

Cook broccoli as directed on package; drain. Stir in mushrooms, margarine, salt and pepper. Heat over low heat, stirring occasionally, until mushrooms are hot, about 5 minutes. Cook spaghetti as directed on package; drain. Toss spaghetti, broccoli mixture, Parmesan cheese and lemon juice. Serve with additional grated Parmesan cheese if desired.

Rigatoni with Pesto Sauce

Rigatoni with Pesto Sauce

8 servings

Cook 1 package (16 ounces) rigatoni macaroni as directed on package; drain. Prepare Pesto Sauce (below); pour over rigatoni. Toss until well coated. Serve with grated Parmesan cheese if desired.

Pesto Sauce

2   cups firmly packed fresh basil leaves
¾   cup grated Parmesan cheese
¾   cup olive oil
2   tablespoons pine nuts
4   cloves garlic

Place all ingredients in blender container. Cover and blend on medium speed, stopping blender occasionally to scrape sides, until smooth, about 3 minutes.

NOTE: Pesto Sauce can be frozen no longer than 6 months. Let stand at room temperature until thawed, at least 4 hours. Toss with hot cooked rigatoni macaroni.

Cheese-Onion Casserole

6 servings

2 medium onions, thinly sliced
1 small green pepper, chopped (about 1/2 cup)
1 jar (4 1/2 ounces) sliced mushrooms, drained
2 tablespoons margarine or butter
2 cups buttermilk baking mix
3/4 cup milk
1 egg
2 cups shredded Swiss cheese (about 8 ounces)
3/4 cup dairy sour cream
1 egg
1/2 teaspoon salt

Heat oven to 400°. Cook and stir onions, green pepper and mushrooms in margarine until tender. Mix baking mix, milk and 1 egg; spread in greased 9 × 9 × 2-inch baking pan. Spread onion mixture on top; sprinkle with cheese. Mix remaining ingredients; pour over cheese. Cook uncovered until golden brown, 30 to 35 minutes.

Cheese and Fruit Pancake

6 servings

2 tablespoons margarine or butter
5 eggs
1 cup all-purpose flour
1 cup milk
1/2 teaspoon salt
1 can (20 ounces) sliced apples, drained
1 can (16 ounces) apricot halves, drained
2 tablespoons packed brown sugar
1/2 teaspoon ground cinnamon
1/2 teaspoon ground nutmeg
1/3 cup chopped walnuts
1 cup shredded Swiss cheese (about 4 ounces)

Heat margarine in 13 × 9 × 2-inch baking pan in 425° oven until melted. Beat eggs, flour, milk and salt with hand beater until smooth; pour into pan. Bake uncovered until puffy and golden brown, 20 to 25 minutes.

Heat apples, apricots, brown sugar, cinnamon and nutmeg until hot; stir in walnuts. Spoon into center of pancake; sprinkle with cheese.

Fiesta Rice

4 servings

1 1/2 cups water
1 teaspoon salt
1/2 teaspoon dry mustard
1/2 teaspoon ground nutmeg
1 1/2 cups uncooked instant rice
8 slices bacon
2 firm bananas, cut diagonally into 1/4-inch slices
1 small green pepper, cut into 1/4-inch strips
1 cup shredded Swiss cheese (about 4 ounces)
1/2 cup milk

Heat water, salt, mustard and nutmeg to boiling. Stir in rice; remove from heat. Cover; let stand until water is absorbed, about 5 minutes.

Fry bacon in 10-inch skillet until crisp; drain on paper towels. Crumble bacon and reserve. Drain fat, reserving 2 tablespoons in skillet. Cook bananas and green pepper in fat over medium heat, stirring occasionally, until bananas are golden brown, 6 to 8 minutes. Stir cheese and milk into rice; heat, stirring occasionally, until hot. Serve banana mixture over rice; sprinkle with bacon.

Three-Cheese Casserole

6 servings

1 cup shredded Monterey Jack cheese
1 cup shredded Cheddar cheese (about 4 ounces)
3/4 cup mayonnaise or salad dressing
1/2 cup sliced green onions (with tops)
1 can (8 ounces) sliced water chestnuts, drained
1 jar (2 ounces) diced pimiento, drained
4 cups hot cooked rice
1/2 cup grated Parmesan cheese

Mix Monterey Jack cheese, Cheddar cheese, mayonnaise, onions, water chestnuts and pimiento. Layer 2 cups of the rice and half of the cheese mixture in greased 2-quart casserole; repeat. Sprinkle with Parmesan cheese. Cook uncovered in 325° oven until hot, about 35 minutes.

Cheese, Bacon and Tomato Pie

Cheese, Bacon and Tomato Pie

6 servings

½ package (11-ounce size) pie crust sticks or mix
1 medium onion, chopped (about ½ cup)
2 tablespoons all-purpose flour
1 medium tomato, thinly sliced
8 slices bacon, crisply fried and crumbled
2 cups shredded mozzarella cheese
      (about 8 ounces)

Have ready at serving time:

2 cups shredded lettuce

Prepare pastry for 9-inch One-Crust Pie as directed on package. Mix onion and flour; sprinkle in pastry-lined pie plate. Top with tomato slices; sprinkle with bacon and cheese. (To serve immediately, continue as directed in TO SERVE.) Cover and refrigerate no longer than 24 hours.

TO SERVE: About 30 minutes before serving, bake Cheese, Bacon and Tomato Pie uncovered in 400° oven until cheese is melted, about 25 minutes. Sprinkle with lettuce.

Spanish Strata

6 servings

6 slices white bread
2 cups shredded Cheddar cheese
¼ cup finely chopped onion
1 teaspoon salt
½ teaspoon Worcestershire sauce
      Dash of cayenne pepper
4 eggs
2½ cups milk

Have ready at serving time:

1 can (16 ounces) stewed tomatoes
1 tablespoon cornstarch
2 tablespoons cold water

Trim crusts from bread; cut bread into 1-inch pieces. Place half of the bread in ungreased 8 × 8 × 2-inch baking dish. Mix cheese, onion, salt, Worcestershire sauce and cayenne pepper. Spread over bread in dish; top with remaining bread. Beat eggs and milk; pour over bread. Cover and refrigerate at least 2 hours but no longer than 24 hours.

TO SERVE: About 1½ hours before serving, cook Spanish Strata uncovered in 325° oven until knife inserted in center comes out clean, about 1¼ hours. Let stand 10 minutes before cutting. Heat tomatoes to boiling. Mix cornstarch and water; stir into tomatoes. Boil and stir 1 minute. Serve with Spanish Strata.

Vegetable Lasagna

8 servings

White Sauce (below)
1   *package (10 ounces) frozen chopped spinach*
2   *cups creamed cottage cheese*
1/2   *cup grated Parmesan cheese*
1   *teaspoon dried basil leaves*
1/2   *teaspoon dried oregano leaves*
1/4   *teaspoon pepper*
12   *lasagna noodles, cooked and drained*
1 1/2   *cups shredded mozzarella cheese*
1   *can (8 ounces) mushroom stems and pieces, drained and coarsely chopped*
2   *medium carrots, coarsely shredded*
1   *medium onion, chopped (about 1/2 cup)*
1   *medium green pepper, chopped (about 1 cup)*

Prepare White Sauce. Rinse frozen spinach under running cold water to separate. Drain; pat dry with paper towels. Mix spinach, cottage cheese, 1/4 cup of the Parmesan cheese, the basil, oregano and pepper. Arrange 4 noodles in ungreased 13 × 9 × 2-inch baking dish. Top with half of the cheese mixture, 1/2 cup of the mozzarella cheese and 4 noodles. Layer mushrooms, carrots, onion and green pepper on noodles. Spread half of the White Sauce over top; sprinkle with 1/2 cup of the mozzarella cheese. Top with remaining noodles, cheese mixture, White Sauce and mozzarella cheese; sprinkle with remaining 1/4 cup Parmesan cheese. (To serve immediately, continue as directed in TO SERVE except — decrease cooking time to about 35 minutes.) Cover and refrigerate no longer than 24 hours.

TO SERVE: About 55 minutes before serving, cook Vegetable Lasagna uncovered in 350° oven until hot and bubbly, about 45 minutes. Let stand 10 minutes before cutting.

White Sauce

1/3   *cup margarine or butter*
1/3   *cup all-purpose flour*
1   *teaspoon salt*
1/8   *teaspoon ground nutmeg*
3   *cups milk*

Heat margarine in 1-quart saucepan over low heat until melted. Stir in flour, salt and nutmeg. Cook over low heat, stirring constantly, until bubbly; remove from heat. Stir in milk. Heat to boiling, stirring constantly. Boil and stir 1 minute; cover and keep warm. (If sauce thickens, beat in small amount milk.)

Eggplant Spaghetti

6 servings

1   *medium eggplant, cut into 1/2-inch cubes*
2   *medium onions, sliced*
2   *cloves garlic, finely chopped*
1/4   *cup olive oil or vegetable oil*
1   *can (28 ounces) pear-shaped tomatoes, Italian-style*
1   *can (15 ounces) tomato sauce*
1   *can (8 ounces) mushroom stems and pieces, drained*
1/2   *cup grated Parmesan cheese*
1   *tablespoon sugar*
1   *teaspoon salt*
1   *teaspoon dried oregano leaves*
1   *teaspoon dried basil leaves*

Have ready at serving time:

1   *package (16 ounces) spaghetti*
1/2   *cup grated Parmesan cheese*

Cook and stir eggplant, onions and garlic in oil in 4-quart Dutch oven until eggplant is tender, about 10 minutes. Stir in tomatoes (with liquid), tomato sauce, mushrooms, 1/2 cup cheese, the sugar, salt, oregano and basil; break up tomatoes with fork. Heat to boiling; reduce heat. Cover and simmer, stirring occasionally, 45 minutes. (To serve immediately, cook spaghetti as directed on package; drain. Pour eggplant sauce over spaghetti; sprinkle with 1/2 cup cheese.) Cover and refrigerate no longer than 3 days.

TO SERVE: About 15 minutes before serving, heat eggplant sauce over medium heat, stirring occasionally, until hot. Cook spaghetti as directed on package; drain. Pour eggplant sauce over spaghetti; sprinkle with 1/2 cup cheese.

Macaroni and Cheese

2 meals - 6 servings each

4 cups uncooked elbow macaroni
  (about 12 ounces)
1 medium onion, chopped (about ½ cup)
⅓ cup margarine or butter
¼ cup all-purpose flour
1 teaspoon salt
¼ teaspoon pepper
4 cups milk
1½ pounds process sharp American cheese,
  cut into ½-inch cubes

Cook macaroni as directed on package; drain. Cook and stir onion in margarine in 4-quart Dutch oven over medium heat until onion is tender. Stir in flour, salt and pepper. Cook over low heat, stirring constantly, until smooth and bubbly; remove from heat. Stir in milk. Heat to boiling, stirring constantly. Boil and stir 1 minute. Stir in cheese; heat until cheese is melted and sauce is smooth. Stir macaroni into cheese sauce. Divide between 2 ungreased 8 × 8 × 2-inch baking pans. (To serve 1 pan immediately, cook uncovered in 375° oven until golden brown, 35 to 40 minutes.) Wrap, label and freeze no longer than 3 months.

TO SERVE: About 1 hour before serving, remove 1 pan Macaroni and Cheese from freezer and unwrap. Cook uncovered in 425° oven until hot and bubbly, about 55 minutes.

PASTA DO-AHEAD TIPS

For approximately 4 cups of cooked pasta, use the following amounts of uncooked pasta: 6 to 7 ounces macaroni (2 cups), 7 to 8 ounces spaghetti or 8 ounces noodles (4 to 5 cups). Hot, cooked pasta should be drained and tossed with 3 tablespoons margarine or butter to keep the pieces separated. If the pasta is to be used in a salad, rinse under running cold water.

Manicotti

2 meals - 6 or 7 servings each

28 uncooked manicotti shells
4 cups ricotta cheese
2 cups shredded mozzarella cheese
1 package (10 ounces) frozen chopped spinach,
  thawed and well drained
3 eggs, slightly beaten
1 teaspoon salt
½ teaspoon freshly ground pepper
½ teaspoon finely shredded lemon peel
1 large clove garlic, finely chopped
  White Sauce (below)
1 cup grated Parmesan cheese

Cook 14 manicotti shells as directed on package. Drain; pat dry on paper towels. Repeat with remaining shells.

Mix ricotta cheese, mozzarella cheese, spinach, eggs, salt, pepper, lemon peel and garlic. Fill each shell with about 3 tablespoons cheese mixture. Divide shells between 2 ungreased 13 × 9 × 2-inch baking dishes. Prepare White Sauce; pour over shells. Sprinkle with Parmesan cheese. (To serve 1 dish immediately, cook uncovered in 350° oven until hot and bubbly, about 40 minutes. Serve with additional grated Parmesan cheese if desired.) Wrap, label and freeze no longer than 1 month.

TO SERVE: About 1 hour 5 minutes before serving, remove 1 dish Manicotti from freezer and unwrap. Heat uncovered in 375° oven until hot, about 1 hour. Serve with additional grated Parmesan cheese if desired.

White Sauce

⅓ cup margarine or butter
⅓ cup all-purpose flour
1 teaspoon salt
4 cups milk

Heat margarine in 2-quart saucepan over low heat until melted. Stir in flour and salt. Cook over low heat, stirring constantly, until smooth and bubbly; remove from heat. Stir in milk. Heat to boiling, stirring constantly. Boil and stir 1 minute.

Eggs and Tomato Stew

6 servings

½ pound bulk Italian sausage
2 cans (16 ounces each) stewed tomatoes
1 can (4 ounces) chopped green chilies, drained
6 eggs
1 cup shredded Cheddar cheese (about 4 ounces)
6 slices bread, toasted and cut into fourths
 Snipped parsley

Cook and stir sausage in 10-inch skillet over medium heat until brown; drain. Stir in tomatoes and chilies. Heat to boiling; reduce heat. Break each egg into measuring cup or saucer; holding cup or saucer close to tomato mixture, slip 1 egg at a time onto tomatoes. Sprinkle with cheese. Cover and simmer until whites of eggs are set and cheese is melted, about 15 minutes. Spoon an egg and the tomato mixture over toast in each serving bowl. Sprinkle with parsley.

Eggs Rarebit

6 servings

1 package (10 ounces) frozen chopped broccoli
1 jar (16 ounces) pasteurized process cheese
 spread
½ teaspoon dry mustard
4 to 6 drops red pepper sauce
8 hard-cooked eggs, sliced
2 medium tomatoes, thinly sliced
3 English muffins, split and toasted, or 6 slices
 bread, toasted

Cook broccoli as directed on package; drain. Add cheese spread, mustard and pepper sauce. Cook over low heat, stirring constantly, until cheese is melted. Gently stir in eggs. Arrange tomato slices on muffin halves; spoon egg mixture over tomatoes. Sprinkle with paprika if desired.

Eggs and Broccoli

6 servings

1	package (10 ounces) frozen chopped broccoli
1/2	teaspoon salt
12	hard-cooked eggs, cut lengthwise into fourths
1	can (11 ounces) condensed Cheddar cheese soup
3/4	cup milk
1	jar (2 ounces) diced pimiento, drained
1	teaspoon parsley flakes
1/2	teaspoon dry mustard
1/4	teaspoon dried basil leaves
1/8	teaspoon onion powder
3	drops red pepper sauce
1	cup crushed corn chips or potato chips

Rinse broccoli in cold water to separate; drain. Spread broccoli in ungreased 12 × 7½ × 2-inch baking dish; sprinkle with salt. Arrange eggs, cut sides up, on broccoli. Mix soup, milk, pimiento, parsley, mustard, basil, onion powder and pepper sauce; heat to boiling. Pour over eggs. Sprinkle with chips. Cook uncovered in 350° oven until hot, 20 to 25 minutes.

Eggs and Macaroni

6 servings

1	can (10¾ ounces) condensed cream of chicken soup
1	cup milk
1	cup water
1	cup uncooked elbow macaroni (3 to 4 ounces)
1	package (10 ounces) frozen mixed vegetables
8	hard-cooked eggs, chopped
1	teaspoon parsley flakes
1/8	teaspoon ground sage
1/3	cup grated Parmesan cheese

Heat soup, milk, water and macaroni to boiling in 3-quart saucepan, stirring occasionally; reduce heat. Cover and simmer, stirring occasionally, 10 minutes. Rinse vegetables in cold water to separate; drain. Stir in vegetables, eggs, parsley and sage. Heat to boiling; reduce heat. Cover and simmer until vegetables are tender, 8 to 10 minutes. Sprinkle with cheese.

DO AHEAD HARD-COOKED EGGS

Hard-cooked eggs are one of the most useful of homemade "fast foods." As insurance against an extra busy day, cook several and keep them in the refrigerator. Mark shells "HC" with a pencil for easy identification.

COLD WATER METHOD: Place eggs in saucepan; add enough cold water to come at least 1 inch above eggs. Heat rapidly to boiling; remove from heat. Cover and let stand 22 to 24 minutes. Immediately cool eggs in cold water to prevent further cooking.

BOILING WATER METHOD: Place eggs in bowl of warm water to prevent shells from cracking. Fill saucepan with enough water to come at least 1 inch above eggs; heat to boiling. Transfer eggs from warm water to boiling water with spoon; reduce heat to below simmering. Cook uncovered 20 minutes. Immediately cool eggs in cold water to prevent further cooking.

Vegetable Omelet

6 servings

1	package (12 ounces) frozen hash brown potatoes
1/4	cup vegetable oil
1	package (4 ounces) sliced fully cooked smoked ham, cut into 1/2-inch strips
1	medium onion, chopped (about 1/2 cup)
6	eggs
1/2	teaspoon salt
1/8	teaspoon pepper
1	can (8 ounces) whole kernel corn, drained
2	tablespoons margarine or butter
	Grated Parmesan cheese

Cook and stir potatoes in oil in 10-inch skillet over medium heat until tender, about 5 minutes. Stir in ham and onion. Cook, stirring occasionally, until onion is tender, about 5 minutes. Beat eggs, salt and pepper. Stir corn and margarine into ham mixture; pour eggs over top. Cover and cook over medium-low heat until eggs are set and light brown on bottom, about 10 minutes. Sprinkle with cheese; cut into wedges.

Blue Cheese Eggs

4 servings

1 medium onion, chopped (about ½ cup)
2 tablespoons margarine or butter
8 eggs, slightly beaten
½ cup milk
2 tablespoons finely crumbled blue cheese
½ teaspoon salt
⅛ teaspoon pepper
8 slices bacon, crisply fried and crumbled

Cook and stir onion in margarine in 10-inch skillet over medium heat until onion is tender. Mix eggs, milk, cheese, salt and pepper; pour into skillet. As mixture begins to set at bottom and side, gently lift cooked portions with spatula so that thin, uncooked portion can flow to bottom. Avoid constant stirring. Cook until eggs are thickened throughout but still moist, about 5 minutes. Stir in bacon.

■ *Microwave Directions:* Place onion and margarine in 2-quart microwaveproof casserole. Microwave uncovered on high (100%) until onion is tender, 3 to 4 minutes. Mix eggs, milk, cheese, salt and pepper; pour into casserole. Microwave uncovered, stirring every 2 minutes, until eggs are set but still moist, 6 to 8 minutes. (Eggs will continue to cook while standing.) Stir in bacon.

Curried Scrambled Eggs

6 servings

1 cup water
1 teaspoon margarine or butter
½ teaspoon salt
1 cup uncooked instant rice
1 medium green pepper, chopped (about 1 cup)
1 medium onion, chopped (about ½ cup)
1 to 1½ teaspoons curry powder
¼ cup margarine or butter
8 eggs, slightly beaten
½ cup milk
½ teaspoon salt
1 medium tomato, chopped (about ¾ cup)

Heat water, 1 teaspoon margarine and ½ teaspoon salt to boiling. Stir in rice; remove from heat. Cover and let stand until water is absorbed, about 5 minutes.

Cook and stir green pepper, onion and curry powder in ¼ cup margarine in 10-inch skillet over medium heat until onion is tender. Mix rice, eggs, milk and ½ teaspoon salt; pour over onion mixture. As mixture begins to set at bottom and side, gently lift cooked portions with spatula so that thin, uncooked portion can flow to bottom. Avoid constant stirring. Cook until eggs are thickened throughout but still moist, 5 to 8 minutes. Sprinkle with tomato. Serve with toasted raisin bread if desired.

Eggs and Corn Scramble

6 servings

2 tablespoons margarine or butter
8 eggs, slightly beaten
1 can (12 ounces) whole kernel corn with peppers
1 cup shredded Cheddar cheese (about 4 ounces)
½ cup milk
½ teaspoon dried basil leaves
½ teaspoon salt
⅛ teaspoon pepper

Heat margarine in 10-inch skillet over medium heat until melted. Mix remaining ingredients; pour into skillet. As mixture begins to set at bottom and side, gently lift cooked portions with spatula so that thin, uncooked portion can flow to bottom. Avoid constant stirring. Cook until eggs are thickened throughout but still moist, 5 to 8 minutes.

■ *Microwave Directions:* Place margarine in 2-quart microwaveproof casserole. Microwave uncovered on high (100%) until melted, 30 to 45 seconds. Mix remaining ingredients; pour into casserole. Microwave, uncovered, stirring every 2 minutes, until eggs are set but still moist, 8 to 10 minutes. (Eggs will continue to cook while standing.)

Eggs and Rice Salad

6 servings

1   package (10 ounces) frozen green peas
8   hard-cooked eggs, coarsely chopped
3   cups cooked rice
2   medium stalks celery, sliced (about 1 cup)
1   small onion, chopped (about 1/4 cup)
4   ounces Swiss or Monterey Jack cheese,
        cut into 1/2-inch cubes
1   jar (2 ounces) diced pimiento, drained
1   cup mayonnaise or salad dressing
1   tablespoon prepared mustard
1   tablespoon lemon juice
1   teaspoon salt
1/8 teaspoon pepper
1/8 teaspoon dried dill weed

Have ready at serving time:

Lettuce leaves

Rinse frozen peas under running cold water to
separate; drain. Mix peas, eggs, rice, celery,
onion, cheese and pimiento. Mix mayonnaise,
mustard, lemon juice, salt, pepper and dill
weed; toss with egg mixture. Cover and
refrigerate at least 4 hours but no longer than
24 hours.

TO SERVE: Just before serving, spoon Eggs
and Rice Salad onto lettuce leaves. Sprinkle
with paprika if desired.

Eggs-stuffing Casserole

8 servings

1   package (6 ounces) stuffing mix
8   hard-cooked eggs, coarsely chopped
3   medium stalks celery, sliced (about 1 1/2 cups)
1   medium onion, chopped (about 1/2 cup)
1/2 cup sliced pimiento-stuffed olives
1/2 cup mayonnaise or salad dressing
1   can (10 3/4 ounces) condensed cream of
        chicken soup
3/4 cup milk

Have ready at serving time:

1   cup shredded Cheddar cheese (about 4 ounces)

Prepare stuffing mix as directed on package.
Mix eggs, celery, onion, olives and mayonnaise. Layer half of the stuffing, the egg mixture and the remaining stuffing in ungreased
12 × 7 1/2 × 2-inch baking dish. Mix soup and
milk until smooth; pour over stuffing. (To
serve immediately, sprinkle with cheese. Cook
uncovered in 350° oven until hot, about 30
minutes.) Cover and refrigerate no longer
than 24 hours.

TO SERVE: About 55 minutes before serving,
sprinkle Eggs-stuffing Casserole with cheese.
Cook uncovered in 350° oven until hot, about
50 minutes.

Scrambled Eggs Pie

6 servings

1   *cup coarsely crushed corn flakes cereal*
2   *tablespoons margarine or butter, melted*
¼   *cup margarine or butter*
8   *eggs*
½   *cup milk*
1   *tablespoon snipped chives*
½   *teaspoon seasoned salt*
⅛   *teaspoon pepper*
6   *slices bacon, crisply fried and crumbled*
3   *slices process American cheese, cut diagonally into halves*

Mix cereal and 2 tablespoons margarine; reserve ¼ cup. Spread remaining cereal mixture in ungreased 9 × 1¼-inch pie plate or quiche dish. Heat ¼ cup margarine in 10-inch skillet over medium heat until melted. Beat eggs, milk, chives, seasoned salt and pepper with hand beater. Pour egg mixture into skillet; add bacon. Cook over low heat, stirring gently, just until eggs are almost set. Quickly spoon into pie plate. Arrange cheese, overlapping slightly, around edge of plate. Sprinkle with reserved cereal mixture. (To serve immediately, heat uncovered in 375° oven until cheese is melted and eggs are firm, 10 to 15 minutes.) Cover and refrigerate no longer than 24 hours.

TO SERVE: About 30 minutes before serving, heat Scrambled Eggs Pie uncovered in 375° oven until eggs are hot and cheese is melted, 20 to 25 minutes.

■ *Microwave Directions:* Mix cereal and 2 tablespoons margarine; reserve ¼ cup. Spread remaining cereal mixture in 9 × 1¼-inch microwaveproof pie plate. Omit ¼ cup margarine. Mix eggs, milk, chives, seasoned salt and pepper with hand beater in 1½-quart microwaveproof casserole; stir in bacon. Cover tightly and microwave on high (100%), stirring every 2 minutes, until eggs are puffy but moist, 6 to 8 minutes. Quickly spoon into pie plate. Arrange cheese, overlapping slightly, around edge of plate; sprinkle with reserved cereal. Microwave uncovered on medium (50%) until cheese is melted, 2 to 3 minutes.

Egg Foo Yung

4 servings - 2 patties each

¼   *cup vegetable oil*
8   *eggs, slightly beaten*
1   *can (16 ounces) bean sprouts, well drained*
1   *can (8 ounces) sliced water chestnuts, well drained*
1   *can (4¼ ounces) shrimp, rinsed, drained and chopped*
1   *can (4 ounces) mushroom stems and pieces, drained and chopped*
2   *green onions (with tops), chopped*

Have ready at serving time:

1   *can (10¾ ounces) condensed chicken broth*
½   *cup water*
2   *tablespoons soy sauce*
2   *tablespoons cornstarch*
2   *tablespoons cold water*

Heat oil in 10-inch skillet over medium-high heat until hot. Mix eggs, bean sprouts, water chestnuts, shrimp, mushrooms and onions. Pour ½ cup egg mixture into skillet. Push cooked egg up over shrimp and vegetables with broad spatula to form a patty. Cook until patty is set and golden brown, about 2 minutes. Turn; cook other side until golden brown, about 2 minutes longer. Repeat with remaining egg mixture. (Add more oil if necessary.) (To serve immediately, keep patties warm in 300° oven. Prepare sauce as directed below; pour over patties.) Wrap, label and freeze no longer than 1 month.

TO SERVE: About 30 minutes before serving, place frozen patties in ungreased 15½ × 10½ × 1-inch jelly roll pan. Heat uncovered in 375° oven until hot, about 25 minutes. Heat broth, water and soy sauce to boiling. Mix cornstarch and water; stir into broth mixture. Cook and stir until thickened, about 15 seconds. Pour over patties.

Chili Beans with Cornmeal Dumplings

4 servings

6 slices bacon, cut up
1 medium onion, chopped (about ½ cup)
1 medium stalk celery, sliced (about ½ cup)
2 cans (15 ounces each) chili beans
¾ cup buttermilk baking mix
⅓ cup cornmeal
½ cup shredded Cheddar cheese
⅓ cup milk

Fry bacon in 3-quart saucepan until crisp; remove bacon with slotted spoon and drain on paper towels. Drain fat, reserving 2 tablespoons in pan. Cook and stir onion and celery in fat until onion is tender. Stir in beans and reserved bacon. Heat to boiling. Mix remaining ingredients until soft dough forms; beat vigorously 20 strokes. Drop dough by 4 spoonfuls onto boiling bean mixture; reduce heat. Simmer uncovered 10 minutes; cover and simmer 10 minutes longer.

Mexican Bean Patties

4 servings

1 can (17 ounces) refried beans
1 egg, slightly beaten
1 cup finely crushed corn chips
1 can (4 ounces) chopped green chilies, drained
1 small onion, chopped (about ¼ cup)
2 tablespoons margarine or butter
2 tablespoons vegetable oil
¼ cup dairy sour cream
¼ cup shredded cheese

Mix beans, egg, chips, chilies and onion. Heat margarine and oil in 10-inch skillet until margarine is melted. Drop bean mixture by 4 spoonfuls into skillet; flatten with spatula to 1-inch thickness. Push in sides to form patties. Cook over medium heat until brown, about 5 minutes on each side. Top patties with sour cream and cheese.

Refried Bean Bake

8 servings

1 can (17 ounces) refried beans
1 medium onion, finely chopped
1 small green pepper, finely chopped
4 eggs
1½ cups shredded Cheddar cheese
1 teaspoon chili powder
⅛ teaspoon garlic powder
1 jar (12 ounces) salsa

Mix beans, onion, green pepper, eggs, ¾ cup of the cheese, the chili powder and garlic powder. Pour into ungreased 9×9×2-inch baking pan; sprinkle with remaining cheese. Cook uncovered in 350° oven until hot and firm, about 30 minutes. Heat salsa, stirring occasionally, until hot; serve with Refried Bean Bake.

Bean and Hominy Stew

6 servings

1 package (10 ounces) frozen sliced okra, rinsed and drained
1 can (30 ounces) kidney beans, drained
1 can (20 ounces) hominy, drained
1 can (16 ounces) whole tomatoes
2 medium stalks celery, thinly sliced
1 tablespoon Worcestershire sauce
½ teaspoon salt
⅛ teaspoon dried dill weed
1½ cups shredded cheese (about 6 ounces)
2 tablespoons imitation bacon

Rinse frozen okra under running cold water to separate; drain. Mix okra, beans, hominy, tomatoes (with liquid), celery, Worcestershire sauce, salt and dill weed in ungreased 2-quart casserole; break up tomatoes with fork. Sprinkle with cheese. Cook uncovered in 350° oven until hot and cheese is melted, about 30 minutes. Sprinkle with imitation bacon. Serve with French bread if desired.

Crunchy Bean Skillet

6 servings

3   cans (16 ounces each) Cannellini beans,
        drained
1   jar (16 ounces) spaghetti sauce
2   medium stalks celery, sliced (about 1 cup)
1/2 cup sliced green onions
1   teaspoon parsley flakes
1   teaspoon dried basil leaves
1/2 teaspoon dried oregano leaves
1   cup shredded mozzarella cheese
        (about 4 ounces)
1/2 cup coarsely chopped walnuts

Mix beans, spaghetti sauce, celery, onions, parsley, basil and oregano in 10-inch skillet; heat to boiling. Sprinkle with cheese. Cover and cook over low heat just until cheese is melted, 3 to 5 minutes. Sprinkle with walnuts.

■ *Microwave Directions:* Mix beans, spaghetti sauce, celery, onions, parsley, basil and oregano in 3-quart microwaveproof casserole. Cover tightly and microwave on high (100%) 4 minutes; stir. Cover and microwave until hot, 4 to 6 minutes longer. Sprinkle with cheese. Cover and let stand until cheese is melted, about 3 minutes. Sprinkle with walnuts.

Beans and Fruit

5 servings

6   slices bacon, cut up
1   medium onion, chopped (about 1/2 cup)
2   cans (20 ounces each) pork and beans
1   can (8 1/4 ounces) crushed pineapple, drained
1   medium green pepper, chopped (about 1 cup)
1/4 cup molasses
1   teaspoon dry mustard
1   medium apple, cored and cut into 5 rings
2   tablespoons packed brown sugar

Fry bacon in 10-inch skillet until crisp; remove bacon with slotted spoon and drain on paper towels. Cook and stir onion in fat until tender. Stir in beans, pineapple, green pepper, molasses, mustard and bacon. Heat to boiling; reduce heat. Arrange apple rings on top; sprinkle with brown sugar. Cover and simmer until apple rings are tender, about 10 minutes.

■ *Microwave Directions:* Place bacon and onion in 2 1/2-quart microwaveproof casserole. Cover loosely and microwave on high (100%) 4 minutes; stir. Cover and microwave until bacon is crisp, 4 to 6 minutes longer; drain. Stir in beans, pineapple, green pepper, molasses and mustard. Cover tightly and microwave until hot, 4 to 6 minutes; stir. Arrange apple rings on top; sprinkle with brown sugar. Cover and microwave until apple rings are tender, 6 to 8 minutes.

Pork and Beans with Onions

4 servings

1   can (12 ounces) pork luncheon meat
2   cans (16 ounces each) pork and beans
1/3 cup catsup
2   tablespoons packed brown sugar
1   tablespoon prepared mustard
1   can (3 ounces) French fried onions

Cut pork into 1/2-inch pieces. Cook and stir pork in 2-quart saucepan until brown. Stir in beans, catsup, brown sugar and mustard. Heat to boiling. Pour into ungreased 1 1/2-quart casserole. Cook uncovered in 400° oven until hot, about 30 minutes. Sprinkle with onions.

■ *Microwave Directions:* Place pork in ungreased 1 1/2-quart microwaveproof casserole. Cover loosely and microwave on high (100%) 4 minutes. Stir in beans, catsup, brown sugar and mustard. Cover and microwave until hot, 5 to 7 minutes. Sprinkle with onions.

Chili Beans and Pasta

8 servings

4	cups water
1	pound dried Great Northern or lima beans
1	medium onion, chopped (about 1/2 cup)
1	tablespoon chili powder
1 1/2	teaspoons salt
2	cloves garlic, finely chopped

Have ready at serving time:

1	can (28 ounces) whole tomatoes
1	can (4 ounces) chopped green chilies
1	cup uncooked small macaroni shells
1	cup shredded Monterey Jack or Cheddar cheese (about 4 ounces)
1/2	cup sliced green onions (with tops)

Heat water and beans to boiling in 4-quart Dutch oven; boil 2 minutes. Remove from heat; cover and let stand 1 hour.

Add enough water to beans to cover if necessary. Add onion, chili powder, salt and garlic. Heat to boiling; reduce heat. Cover and simmer until tender, about 1 1/2 hours (do not boil or beans will burst). (To serve immediately, continue as directed in **TO SERVE**.) Cover and refrigerate no longer than 5 days.

TO SERVE: About 30 minutes before serving, heat beans to boiling. Stir in tomatoes (with liquid), chilies (with liquid) and macaroni; break up tomatoes with fork. Heat to boiling; reduce heat. Cover and simmer until macaroni is tender, about 15 minutes. Sprinkle each serving with cheese and onions.

Italian Lima Beans

6 servings

4	cups water
1	pound dried lima beans (about 2 cups)
2	teaspoons salt

Have ready at serving time:

1	medium onion, finely chopped
1	medium green pepper, chopped (about 1 cup)
1	can (15 ounces) tomato sauce special
1/2	cup sliced ripe olives
1/4	cup grated Parmesan or Romano cheese
1	teaspoon dried basil leaves

Heat water, beans and salt to boiling in 4-quart Dutch oven; boil 2 minutes. Remove from heat; cover and let stand 1 hour.

Add enough water to beans to cover if necessary. Heat to boiling; reduce heat. Cover and simmer, stirring occasionally, until tender, 1 1/4 to 1 1/2 hours (do not boil or beans will burst). Add more water during cooking if necessary. (To serve immediately, continue as directed in **TO SERVE** except — decrease cooking time to about 30 minutes.) Cover and refrigerate no longer than 3 days.

TO SERVE: About 45 minutes before serving, drain beans. Mix beans, onion, green pepper, tomato sauce, ripe olives, cheese and basil in ungreased 2-quart casserole. Cook uncovered in 375° oven until hot and bubbly, about 40 minutes.

Vegetable Bean Salad

6 servings

1   *package (10 ounces) frozen cauliflower*
    Herb Dressing (below)
2   *cans (16 ounces each) garbanzo beans, drained*
2   *medium zucchini, thinly sliced*
2   *medium tomatoes, coarsely chopped*
1/4 *cup snipped parsley*
2   *tablespoons capers*

Have ready at serving time:

1/2 *cup grated Parmesan cheese*
    Lettuce leaves
3   *hard-cooked eggs, cut into wedges*

Rinse frozen cauliflower under running cold water to separate; drain. Prepare Herb Dressing; toss with cauliflower, beans, zucchini, tomatoes, parsley and capers. Cover and refrigerate at least 4 hours but no longer than 24 hours.

Herb Dressing

1/3 *cup olive oil or vegetable oil*
3   *tablespoons wine vinegar*
1   *teaspoon salt*
1/2 *teaspoon dried tarragon leaves*
1/4 *teaspoon dried basil leaves*
1   *large clove garlic, crushed*

Shake all ingredients in covered container.

TO SERVE: At serving time, toss bean mixture with cheese; spoon onto lettuce leaves. Garnish with egg wedges.

Boston Baked Beans

2 meals - 4 servings each

6   *cups water*
1½   *pounds dried navy or pea beans (about 3 cups)*
1   *large onion, sliced*
1/4 *cup thinly sliced salt pork (with rind)*
3/4 *cup molasses*
1/4 *cup packed brown sugar*
1   *teaspoon salt*
1   *teaspoon dry mustard*
1/8 *teaspoon pepper*

Heat water and beans to boiling in 4-quart Dutch oven; boil 2 minutes. Remove from heat; cover and let stand 1 hour.

Add enough water to beans to cover if necessary. Heat to boiling; reduce heat. Cover and simmer until tender, 1 to 1½ hours (do not boil or beans will burst). Drain beans, reserving liquid.

Layer beans, onion and pork in ungreased 4-quart bean pot, casserole or Dutch oven. Mix molasses, brown sugar, salt, mustard, pepper and reserved bean liquid; pour over beans. Add enough water to almost cover beans. Cover and cook in 350° oven, stirring occasionally, 3 hours. Uncover and cook until beans are desired consistency, about 30 minutes longer. (Can be served immediately.) Divide between two 8 × 8 × 2-inch baking pans. Wrap, label and freeze no longer than 2 months.

TO SERVE: About 45 minutes before serving, remove 1 pan Boston Baked Beans from freezer and unwrap. Heat uncovered in 350° oven, stirring occasionally, until hot, about 40 minutes.

Salads, Vegetables & Serve-withs

1. Lettuce and Mushroom Salad, 2. Golden Breadsticks,
3. Rice-Stuffed Tomatoes

German Potato Salad

6 servings

4   slices bacon, cut up
1   medium onion, chopped (about ½ cup)
2   cans (16 ounces each) sliced potatoes, drained
¼   cup vinegar
1   tablespoon sugar
½   teaspoon salt
⅛   teaspoon pepper

Fry bacon in 10-inch skillet over medium heat until crisp. Remove bacon with slotted spoon; drain on paper towels. Cook and stir onion in bacon fat until tender. Stir in bacon and the remaining ingredients. Cook uncovered, stirring occasionally, until potatoes are hot and sauce is thickened, about 5 minutes. Garnish with snipped parsley and hard-cooked egg wedges if desired.

■ *Microwave Directions:* Decrease vinegar to 2 tablespoons. Place bacon in 1½-quart microwaveproof casserole. Cover with paper towel and microwave on high (100%) until crisp, 4 to 6 minutes; drain on paper towels. Add onion to bacon fat in casserole. Cover tightly and microwave until onion is crisp-tender, 2 to 3 minutes. Stir in bacon and the remaining ingredients. Cover and microwave 3 minutes; stir. Cover and microwave until potatoes are hot, 3 to 5 minutes longer. Garnish with snipped parsley and hard-cooked egg wedges if desired.

Tomato and Cheese Salads

6 servings

3   large tomatoes, each cut into 6 slices
     Bottled Italian salad dressing
¾   cup shredded Cheddar or Swiss cheese
2   green onions (with tops), thinly sliced

Arrange 3 tomato slices on each of 6 salad plates; drizzle with dressing. Sprinkle with cheese and onions.

Broiled Lettuce Salads

6 servings

1   firm large head iceberg lettuce, cut into 6 slices
2   medium tomatoes, each cut into 6 slices
¾   cup bottled buttermilk salad dressing
½   cup shredded Cheddar or process American cheese
¼   cup sliced green onions (with tops)

Place lettuce slices on ungreased cookie sheet. Place 2 tomato slices on each lettuce slice. Spoon about 1 tablespoon dressing onto each tomato slice; sprinkle with cheese. Set oven control to broil and/or 550°. Broil salads with tops 2 to 3 inches from heat just until dressing and cheese bubble, about 2 minutes. Sprinkle with onions.

Easy Caesar Salad

8 servings

3   anchovy fillets
⅓   cup bottled Caesar salad dressing
⅓   cup grated Parmesan cheese
1   large bunch romaine, torn into bite-size pieces (about 10 cups)
1   cup onion-garlic flavored croutons.

Mash anchovies with fork in 3-qt. bowl. Stir in dressing and cheese; toss with romaine and croutons until coated with dressing.

Lettuce and Mushroom Salad

8 servings

2 heads Boston lettuce, torn into bite-size pieces
(about 8 cups)
8 ounces mushrooms, sliced
Mustard Dressing (below)

Place lettuce in bowl; top with mushrooms. Serve with Mustard Dressing and, if desired, freshly ground black pepper.

Mustard Dressing

1/2 cup plus 2 tablespoons olive oil or vegetable oil
2 tablespoons Dijon-style mustard
2 tablespoons vinegar

Place all ingredients in blender container. Cover and blend on high speed until mixture begins to thicken, about 15 seconds.

Wilted Lettuce Salad

6 servings

1 large bunch leaf lettuce, torn into medium-size pieces (about 12 cups)
4 slices bacon, cut up
1 medium onion, chopped (about 1/2 cup)
1 tablespoon sugar
2 tablespoons vinegar
1/2 teaspoon salt
1/8 teaspoon pepper

Place lettuce in 3-quart bowl. Fry bacon in 8-inch skillet over medium heat until crisp. Remove bacon with slotted spoon; sprinkle over lettuce.

Cook and stir onion in bacon fat until tender; remove from heat. Stir in remaining ingredients. Heat to boiling; immediately pour over lettuce. Toss just until lettuce is wilted.

Antipasto Toss

8 servings

1/2 cup bottled creamy Italian salad dressing
1/4 cup grated Parmesan cheese
6 cups bite-size pieces salad greens
1 can (14 ounces) artichoke hearts, drained and cut into fourths
1 package (5 ounces) sliced pepperoni, cut up
2 cups cherry tomatoes
1/2 cup pitted ripe olives

Mix dressing and cheese; toss with remaining ingredients. Refrigerate any remaining salad.

Tossed Salad with Walnuts

6 servings

1/2 cup coarsely chopped walnuts
1/4 cup vegetable oil
1/2 teaspoon salt
3 tablespoons tarragon wine vinegar
1 teaspoon sugar
4 cups bite-size pieces salad greens
1 small red onion, thinly sliced

Cook and stir walnuts in oil in 8-inch skillet until toasted, about 4 minutes; remove from heat. Remove walnuts with slotted spoon; drain on paper towels. Sprinkle with salt. Stir vinegar and sugar into oil in skillet; toss with salad greens and onion until well coated. Sprinkle with walnuts.

Tossed Salad Chart

For a salad for 6 to 8 servings, start with about 12 cups crisp salad greens. Add some vegetables, fruit, meat, fish or cheese and toss with ⅓ to ½ cup of your favorite dressing. Top with one or two items to add interest and flavor.

START WITH Select 1 or more to total 12 cups	Bibb Lettuce Boston Lettuce Curly Endive Endive	Escarole Iceberg Lettuce Leaf Lettuce Red Leaf Lettuce	Romaine Spinach Watercress

ADD
Select 1 or more
to total 1½ cups
	FRESH VEGETABLES:
	Alfalfa Sprouts
	Bean Sprouts
	Broccoli Flowerets
	Carrots, thinly sliced
	  or shredded
	Cauliflowerets
	Celery, sliced or
	  chopped
	Cucumbers, sliced or
	  cubed
	Green or Red Peppers
	Mushrooms, sliced
	Onions, sliced or
	  chopped
	Radishes, sliced
	Tomatoes, cut into
	  wedges or coarsely
	  chopped
	Zucchini, sliced or
	  chopped
		MARINATED VEGETABLES:
		Artichoke Hearts
		Beets
		Brussels Sprouts
		Carrots
		Chili Peppers, chopped
		Green Beans
		Mixed Beans
		Mixed Vegetables
		Mushrooms
		FRUITS:
		Apples, cut into wedges
		  or chopped
		Avocados, sliced or
		  cubed
		Bananas, sliced
		Grapefruit Sections
		Grapes, whole or
		  halves
		Nectarines
			Orange Sections
			Peaches, sliced or cubed
			Pears, sliced or cubed
			Plums, sliced
			MEAT, FISH AND CHEESE:
			Chicken, Cold Cuts,
			  Ham, Roast Beef,
			  Tongue or Turkey,
			  cut into strips
			  or cubes
			Sausages, thinly sliced
			  or cubed
			Shrimp, Crabmeat or
			  Lobster, cut up,
			Tuna or Salmon
			Cheddar, Colby,
			  Monterey Jack or
			  Swiss Cheese, cut into
			  strips or cubes

TOP WITH
Select 1 or more
	Almonds, Cashews,
	  Peanuts, Pecans or
	  Walnuts
	Anchovies
	Bacon, crisply fried and
	  crumbled
	Blue Cheese, crumbled
		Carrot Curls
		Cherry Tomatoes
		Chili Peppers
		Cocktail Onions
		Croutons
		French Fried Onions
			Hard-Cooked Eggs,
			  sliced or chopped
			Olives, pitted whole or
			  sliced
			Parmesan Cheese, grated
			Sesame Seeds, toasted
			Sunflower Nuts

ABOUT SALAD GREENS

The most successful salads are composed of fresh, dry salad greens and are often a combination of several kinds — dark and pale green, crisp and tender, bland and tangy. Some shredded red cabbage and available fresh herbs add interest.

Several hours before serving, wash greens thoroughly under running cold water. Shake off moisture; then toss in a towel, dry in a salad spinner or blot with paper towels. Return greens to plastic bag in refrigerator, allowing them to regain their crispness.

With the exception of iceberg lettuce, which can be shredded or served as lettuce cups or wedges, salad greens should be torn rather than cut into bite-size pieces. At serving time, pour on only enough dressing to coat all ingredients lightly; then toss.

Tossed Fruit Salad

6 servings

Honey Dressing (below)
6   cups bite-size pieces salad greens
4   plums, each cut into 8 wedges
2   nectarines, each cut into 8 wedges
1/2 cup shredded Swiss cheese

Prepare Honey Dressing; toss with greens, fruits and cheese.

Honey Dressing

2   tablespoons vegetable oil
1   tablespoon lemon juice
1   tablespoon honey
1/2 teaspoon salt

Shake in tightly covered container.

California Salads

4 servings

2   oranges, pared and sectioned
1   avocado, sliced
1   cup alfalfa sprouts
     Bottled sweet-and-sour salad dressing
1/4 cup sliced green onions (with tops)

Arrange orange sections and avocado on 4 salad plates. Top each with 1/4 cup alfalfa sprouts. Drizzle with dressing; sprinkle with onions. Sprinkle with chopped toasted almonds if desired.

Fruit and Spinach Salad

6 to 8 servings

1   tablespoon sesame seed
12   ounces spinach, torn into bite-size pieces
     (about 12 cups)
2   medium bananas, cut into 1/2-inch slices
1   can (15 1/4 ounces) pineapple chunks, drained
1   can (11 ounces) mandarin orange segments,
     drained
1/3 cup bottled sweet-and-spicy French salad
     dressing

Cook sesame seed over medium heat, stirring constantly, until golden brown; reserve. Mix spinach, bananas, pineapple and orange segments; toss with dressing. Sprinkle with reserved sesame seed.

Mixed Fruit Salad

6 servings

2   cups blueberries or strawberry halves
2   papayas or 1 small cantaloupe, cut up
2   kiwi, sliced
     Poppy Seed Dressing (below)

Mix blueberries, papayas and kiwi; toss with Poppy Seed Dressing. Serve on salad greens and sprinkle with toasted almonds if desired.

Poppy Seed Dressing

Shake 1/2 cup red wine vinegar and oil dressing, 2 tablespoons honey and 1/2 teaspoon poppy seed in tightly covered container.

EASY FRUIT SALADS

Arrange fruits on crisp salad greens and serve with your favorite sweet fruit dressing.

Avocado slices, orange sections and banana slices topped with cranberry sauce.

Apple slices, pineapple chunks, mandarin orange segments and seedless green grapes.

Orange sections, strawberries, seedless green grapes and banana slices.

Orange slices and thin slices of Bermuda onion sprinkled with snipped parsley.

Seedless grapes, chopped celery, maraschino cherry halves and coarsely chopped nuts.

Cantaloupe slices, grapefruit sections and strawberry halves.

Spiced apple rings, canned pear slices and pitted dark sweet cherries sprinkled with chopped pecans.

Mandarin orange segments, banana slices, apple slices and chopped dates.

Clockwise from top: California Salads, Mixed Fruit Salad, Tossed Fruit Salad, and Fruit and Spinach Salad

Brussels Sprouts Mimosa

6 servings

2   packages (10 ounces each) frozen baby
       Brussels sprouts
2   hard-cooked eggs, coarsely chopped
½   cup bottled Italian salad dressing

Have ready at serving time:

   Mustard Sauce (below)
4   slices bacon, crisply fried and crumbled

Cook Brussels sprouts as directed on package; drain. Toss sprouts, eggs and dressing. Cover and refrigerate at least 8 hours but no longer than 24 hours.

Prepare Mustard Sauce; spoon over sprouts. Sprinkle with bacon.

Mustard Sauce

½   cup mayonnaise or salad dressing
2   teaspoons dry mustard
1   teaspoon prepared horseradish

Mix all ingredients.

Marinated Whole Tomatoes

6 servings

6   medium tomatoes, peeled
1   small onion, finely chopped
¾   cup vinegar
½   cup vegetable oil
2   teaspoons sugar
½   teaspoon red pepper sauce
1   clove garlic, crushed

Place tomatoes in 9 × 9 × 2-inch baking dish. Mix remaining ingredients; spoon onto tomatoes. Cover and refrigerate, turning occasionally, at least 8 hours but no longer than 24 hours. Sprinkle with parsley if desired.

Curried Vegetable Salad

6 servings

1   carton (6 ounces) plain yogurt
1   tablespoon chutney
1   teaspoon curry powder
½   teaspoon salt
2   medium cucumbers, thinly sliced
2   medium tomatoes, chopped (about 1½ cups)
1   small green pepper, chopped (about ½ cup)
1   small onion, chopped (about ¼ cup)

Mix yogurt, chutney, curry powder and salt in 3-quart bowl; toss with remaining ingredients. Cover and refrigerate at least 8 hours but no longer than 24 hours. Sprinkle with flaked or shredded coconut if desired.

Italian Red Pepper Salad

6 servings

¼   cup vegetable oil
2   tablespoons vinegar
½   teaspoon dried basil leaves
½   teaspoon dried oregano leaves
¼   teaspoon salt
1   clove garlic, crushed
2   medium red or green peppers, cut into thin rings
1   small onion, thinly sliced
4   ounces mushrooms, sliced

Mix oil, vinegar, basil, oregano, salt and garlic. Stir in remaining ingredients. Cover and refrigerate at least 8 hours but no longer than 48 hours. Serve on salad greens if desired.

Carrot Salad

8 servings

½ cup bottled French salad dressing
1 teaspoon prepared mustard
¼ teaspoon Worcestershire sauce
2 jars (16 ounces each) whole baby
 carrots, drained
1 small green pepper, chopped (about ½ cup)
1 small onion, thinly sliced

Mix dressing, mustard and Worcestershire sauce in 2-quart bowl. Stir in vegetables until coated with dressing. Cover and refrigerate at least 8 hours but no longer than 48 hours.

Lima Bean Salad

6 servings

½ cup mayonnaise or salad dressing
1 tablespoon prepared mustard
¼ teaspoon salt
1 can (16 ounces) lima beans, drained
1 jar (2 ounces) diced pimiento, drained
1 large stalk celery, chopped (about ¾ cup)
⅓ cup sliced green onions (with tops)

Mix mayonnaise, mustard and salt in 1½-quart bowl; toss with remaining ingredients. Cover and refrigerate at least 2 hours but no longer than 48 hours.

Easy Cucumber Salad

6 servings

½ cup mayonnaise or salad dressing
½ teaspoon salt
¼ teaspoon celery seed
⅛ teaspoon pepper
2 medium cucumbers, thinly sliced
1 small onion, thinly sliced

Mix all ingredients. Cover and refrigerate at least 8 hours but no longer than 24 hours.

Carrot Salad

Freezer Cabbage Salad

3 salads - 4 servings each

1 large head cabbage, shredded (about 6 cups)
1 teaspoon salt
1¼ cups sugar
1 cup vinegar
¼ cup water
½ teaspoon dry mustard
½ teaspoon paprika
1 medium green pepper, chopped (about 1 cup)
1 jar (2 ounces) diced pimiento, drained

Sprinkle cabbage with salt in 3-quart bowl; let stand 2 hours. Heat sugar, vinegar, water, mustard and paprika to boiling. Boil 1 minute; cool. Drain cabbage; stir in green pepper and pimiento. Toss vinegar mixture with vegetables. Divide among three 1-pint freezer containers. Cover, label and freeze no longer than 2 months.

TO SERVE: About 4 hours before serving, remove 1 container Freezer Cabbage Salad from freezer. Thaw at room temperature.

Freezer Cucumber Salad

3 salads - 4 servings each

6 cucumbers, thinly sliced
2 teaspoons salt
½ cup sugar
½ cup vinegar
¼ cup vegetable oil
1 jar (2 ounces) diced pimiento, drained
1 teaspoon dried dill weed

Sprinkle cucumbers with salt; let stand 2 hours. Heat sugar, vinegar and oil to boiling; cool. Drain cucumbers; stir in pimiento and dill weed. Toss vegetables with vinegar mixture. Divide among three 1-pint freezer containers. Cover, label and freeze no longer than 2 months.

TO SERVE: About 4 hours before serving, remove 1 container Freezer Cucumber Salad from freezer. Thaw at room temperature.

Crunchy Fruit Salad

6 servings

2 medium bananas
2 medium oranges, pared and sectioned
1 cup strawberries, cut into halves

Have ready at serving time:

½ cup dairy sour cream
1 tablespoon honey
1 tablespoon orange juice
1 cup Granola (page 142)

Slice bananas into 1-quart bowl. Cover completely with oranges and strawberries. Cover and refrigerate at least 1 hour but no longer than 24 hours.

TO SERVE: Just before serving, mix sour cream, honey and orange juice. Fold into fruit until well coated. Sprinkle with Granola.

24-Hour Salad

8 servings

Fruit Salad Dressing (below)
1 can (20 ounces) pineapple chunks, drained (reserve 2 tablespoons syrup)
1 can (17 ounces) apricot halves, drained
1 can (16 ounces) pitted red tart cherries, drained
1 can (11 ounces) mandarin orange segments, drained
1 cup miniature marshmallows

Prepare Fruit Salad Dressing; toss with remaining ingredients. Cover and refrigerate at least 12 hours but no longer than 24 hours.

Fruit Salad Dressing

1 envelope (1½ ounces) whipped topping mix
¼ cup milk
2 tablespoons lemon juice
2 tablespoons reserved pineapple syrup
Dash of salt

Beat topping mix and milk on high speed until soft peaks form. Beat until light and fluffy, about 2 minutes. Stir in remaining ingredients.

Molded Apple Salad

Molded Apple Salad

6 servings

1   cup boiling water
1   package (3 ounces) cherry-flavored gelatin
1   cup cranberry juice
1   tablespoon lemon juice
2   tart apples, chopped (about 2½ cups)
½   cup thinly sliced celery
⅓   cup chopped nuts, if desired

Have ready at serving time:

   Lettuce leaves

Pour boiling water on gelatin in 2-quart bowl; stir until gelatin is dissolved. Stir in cranberry juice and lemon juice. Refrigerate until cool. Fold in remaining ingredients. Pour into 3½-cup mold. Refrigerate until firm, at least 4 hours but no longer than 3 days.

TO SERVE: At serving time, unmold Molded Apple Salad onto lettuce leaves. Serve with mayonnaise or salad dressing if desired.

Blueberry Delight

9 servings

1   cup boiling water
1   envelope (1 tablespoon) unflavored gelatin
1   can (21 ounces) blueberry pie filling
1   cup boiling water
1   package (3 ounces) lemon-flavored gelatin
1   package (3 ounces) cream cheese, softened
⅓   cup mayonnaise or salad dressing
1   cup miniature marshmallows

Pour 1 cup boiling water on unflavored gelatin in 1-quart bowl; stir until gelatin is dissolved. Stir in pie filling; pour into ungreased 9 × 9 × 2-inch baking pan. Refrigerate until firm, about 1 hour.

Pour 1 cup boiling water on lemon-flavored gelatin in 2-quart bowl; stir until gelatin is dissolved. Refrigerate until slightly thickened but not set. Stir in cream cheese and mayonnaise; beat on medium speed until light and fluffy. Stir in marshmallows; pour on gelatin in pan. Refrigerate until firm, at least 3 hours but no longer than 24 hours.

Cabbage and Carrots

6 servings

1   tablespoon cornstarch
1   tablespoon cold water
¼   cup vegetable oil
1   medium head cabbage (about 1 pound),
        cut into 1½-inch pieces
2   medium carrots, shredded (about 1 cup)
4   green onions (with tops), sliced
2   cloves garlic, finely chopped
¼   cup chili sauce
1   teaspoon salt
½   cup chicken broth

Mix cornstarch and water. Heat oil in 12-inch skillet or wok until hot. Add cabbage, carrots, onions and garlic; cook and stir 1 minute. Add chili sauce and salt; cook and stir 1 minute. Stir in broth. Heat to boiling; stir in cornstarch mixture. Cook and stir until thickened, about 10 seconds.

Sweet-and-Sour Beets

8 servings

½   cup vinegar
⅓   cup sugar
½   teaspoon grated orange peel
¼   cup orange juice
¼   teaspoon salt
2   cans (16 ounces each) sliced beets, drained

Heat vinegar, sugar, orange peel, orange juice and salt to boiling in 2-quart saucepan, stirring occasionally; reduce heat. Simmer uncovered 5 minutes. Stir in beets; heat until hot. Sprinkle with snipped parsley if desired.

SWEET-AND-SOUR BEET SALAD: After stirring in beets, cover and refrigerate at least 8 hours. Serve on salad greens; sprinkle with snipped parsley if desired.

Sautéed Artichoke Hearts

4 servings

2   slices bacon, cut up
1   can (14 ounces) artichoke hearts, drained
        and cut into halves
1   teaspoon lemon juice

Fry bacon in 10-inch skillet until partially cooked, about 1½ minutes. Add artichokes; cook and stir until hot, about 3 minutes. Stir in lemon juice; cook 10 seconds longer.

Italian-Style Green Beans

6 servings

1½   pounds green beans*
1   small red onion, thinly sliced
1   cup pitted small ripe olives
½   cup bottled Italian salad dressing
1   large tomato, chopped (about 1 cup)

Cut beans crosswise into 1-inch pieces. Heat beans and 1 inch salted water (½ teaspoon salt to 1 cup water) to boiling. Cook uncovered 5 minutes. Cover and cook until tender, 5 to 10 minutes; drain. Stir in onion, olives and dressing. Cook uncovered over medium heat just until onion is tender, about 3 minutes. Sprinkle with tomato.

*2 packages (10 ounces each) frozen cut green beans, cooked and drained, can be substituted for the fresh green beans.

GREEN BEANS VINAIGRETTE: After draining beans, stir in remaining ingredients. Cover and refrigerate at least 8 hours but no longer than 48 hours.

◾ *Microwave Directions:* Place beans and ¼ cup water in 3-quart microwaveproof casserole. Cover tightly and microwave on high (100%) 6 minutes; stir. Cover and microwave until tender, 5 to 7 minutes longer. Let stand 1 minute; drain. Stir in onion, olives and dressing. Microwave uncovered until onion is tender, 1 to 3 minutes. Sprinkle with tomato.

Southern Corn

4 servings

1 package (10 ounces) frozen whole kernel corn
¼ cup margarine or butter
1 tablespoon packed brown sugar
2 tablespoons whiskey
⅓ cup coarsely chopped pecans

Cook and stir corn in margarine in 10-inch skillet over medium-high heat until tender, about 5 minutes. Stir in brown sugar and whiskey. Cook uncovered, stirring constantly, until mixture thickens, about 2 minutes. Sprinkle with pecans.

Carrots and Pineapple

6 servings

8 medium carrots
2 tablespoons margarine or butter
2 tablespoons packed brown sugar
1 teaspoon salt
1 can (20 ounces) pineapple chunks, drained
¼ teaspoon dried chervil leaves
½ cup dairy sour cream
2 tablespoons water

Cut carrots into strips, each about 3 × ½ inch. Heat 1 inch salted water (½ teaspoon salt to 1 cup water) to boiling. Add carrots. Cover and cook until crisp-tender, about 5 minutes; drain.

Heat margarine in 10-inch skillet over medium-high heat until melted. Add carrots, brown sugar and salt. Cook, stirring occasionally, 5 minutes. Stir in pineapple and chervil. Heat until pineapple is hot; remove from heat. Stir in sour cream and water.

Creamed Cucumbers

6 to 8 servings

4 large cucumbers (about 2½ pounds)
1 can (10¾ ounces) condensed cream of chicken soup
1 can (8 ounces) sliced water chestnuts, drained
⅓ cup milk
¼ teaspoon dried dill weed
1 jar (2 ounces) diced pimiento, drained

Cut cucumbers lengthwise into halves; remove seeds. Cut each half into ½-inch slices. Mix cucumbers, soup, water chestnuts and milk in 3-quart saucepan. Heat to boiling; reduce heat. Cover and simmer until cucumbers are tender, about 6 minutes. Stir in dill weed and pimiento.

Microwave Directions: Prepare cucumbers as directed. Mix cucumbers, soup, water chestnuts and ¼ cup milk in 3-quart microwave-proof dish. Cover tightly and microwave on high (100%) 3 minutes; stir. Cover; microwave until cucumbers are tender, 3 to 5 minutes longer. Stir in dill weed and pimiento.

Creamed Cucumbers

Mushrooms and Broccoli

6 servings

1½ pounds broccoli
2 tablespoons cornstarch
2 tablespoons cold water
¼ cup vegetable oil
8 ounces small mushrooms
1 medium onion, thinly sliced
2 cloves garlic, finely chopped
½ teaspoon salt
½ cup chicken broth
2 tablespoons soy sauce

Cut broccoli into 1-inch pieces. Cut lengthwise gashes in stems thicker than 1 inch. Mix cornstarch and water.

Heat oil in 12-inch skillet or wok until hot. Cook and stir mushrooms, onion and garlic in oil until onion is tender; remove with slotted spoon and reserve. Add broccoli and salt; cook and stir 2 minutes. Stir in broth and soy sauce. Heat to boiling; reduce heat. Cover and simmer 5 minutes. Add reserved vegetables. Heat to boiling; stir in cornstarch mixture. Cook and stir until thickened, about 10 seconds.

Onions with Blue Cheese

6 servings

1 package (16 ounces) frozen whole
    small onions*
1 cup bottled blue cheese salad dressing
6 slices bacon, crisply fried and crumbled
¼ teaspoon dried dill weed

Cook onions as directed on package; drain. Place onions in 9-inch pie plate or heatproof serving dish. Mix remaining ingredients; spoon over onions. Set oven control to broil and/or 550°. Broil onions with tops 3 to 5 inches from heat until topping is light brown and bubbly, 2 to 3 minutes.

*2 cans (16 ounces each) whole small onions, heated and drained, can be substituted for the frozen onions.

Peas with Sesame Butter

4 servings

1 package (10 ounces) frozen green peas
¼ cup margarine or butter
1 tablespoon sesame seed
1 teaspoon sugar
¼ teaspoon salt

Cook peas as directed on package; drain. Cook remaining ingredients over medium heat, stirring constantly, until golden brown; pour over peas.

Baked Potato Slices

4 to 6 servings

4 medium potatoes, cut lengthwise into
    ¼-inch slices
2 tablespoons margarine or butter, softened
½ cup finely crushed corn flake cereal
1 teaspoon salt

Score cut surface of each potato slice in diamond pattern; place on greased cookie sheet. Brush potatoes with margarine. Mix cereal and salt; sprinkle over potatoes. Cook uncovered in 375° oven until tender and golden brown, about 30 minutes.

Chantilly Potatoes

4 to 5 servings

Instant mashed potatoes for 4 servings
½ cup whipping cream
1 teaspoon sugar
½ teaspoon onion powder
⅓ cup grated Parmesan cheese

Prepare potatoes as directed on package for 4 servings. Spoon into ungreased 1½-quart casserole. Beat whipping cream, sugar and onion powder in 1-quart chilled bowl until stiff; spread over potatoes. Sprinkle with cheese. Cook uncovered in 350° oven until hot and golden brown, about 30 minutes. Sprinkle with snipped parsley if desired.

Potato Puffs

8 servings

¾ cup water
¼ cup margarine or butter
1 teaspoon instant minced onion
⅛ teaspoon salt
½ cup instant mashed potatoes (dry)
¼ cup all-purpose flour
2 eggs

Have ready at serving time:

Dairy sour cream
Chopped green onions or snipped chives

Heat oven to 400°. Heat water, margarine, onion and salt to rolling boil in 1½-quart saucepan. Stir in potatoes and flour. Stir vigorously over low heat just until mixture forms a ball, about 1 minute. Remove from heat. Beat in eggs until smooth. Drop dough by heaping tablespoonfuls onto ungreased cookie sheet.

Cook until puffed and golden, about 30 minutes. (Can be served immediately.) Cool; cover and refrigerate no longer than 2 days.

TO SERVE: About 15 minutes before serving, heat Potato Puffs uncovered on ungreased cookie sheet in 425° oven until hot, about 10 minutes. Serve with sour cream and onions.

Mexican Hash Browns

4 to 6 servings

1 package (5.5 ounces) hash brown potato mix with onions
1 can (4 ounces) chopped green chilies, drained
1 cup shredded Monterey Jack cheese (about 4 ounces)
½ teaspoon salt
3 tablespoons margarine or butter

Cover potatoes with boiling water; let stand 5 minutes. Drain thoroughly. Layer half each of the potatoes, chilies and cheese in ungreased 8×8×2-inch or shallow 8-inch baking dish. Sprinkle with half of the salt; dot with half of the margarine. Repeat with remaining ingredients. (To serve immediately, cover and cook in 350° oven 20 minutes. Uncover and cook until golden, about 10 minutes longer.) Cover and refrigerate no longer than 24 hours.

TO SERVE: About 35 minutes before serving, cook Mexican Hash Browns covered in 350° oven 20 minutes. Uncover and cook until golden brown, about 15 minutes longer.

HOT MEXICAN HASH BROWNS: Substitute 1 can (4 ounces) chopped jalapeño peppers, drained, for the chilies.

Potato-Almond Patties

6 servings

1   cup water
1/3 cup milk
2   tablespoons margarine or butter
1/2 teaspoon salt
1 1/3 cups instant mashed potatoes (dry)
1/3 cup chopped green onions (with tops)
2   tablespoons finely chopped almonds
2   tablespoons all-purpose flour

Have ready at serving time:

2   tablespoons margarine or butter
2   tablespoons vegetable oil

Heat water, milk, margarine and salt to boiling in 2-quart saucepan; remove from heat. Stir in potatoes and onions. Whip with fork until thick; cool. Shape potato mixture into 6 patties, each about 3 inches in diameter. Mix almonds and flour; coat each patty with almond mixture. (To serve immediately, continue as directed in TO SERVE.) Cover and refrigerate no longer than 48 hours.

TO SERVE: Heat margarine and oil in 10-inch skillet until hot. Cook Potato-Almond Patties, turning once, until golden brown and hot, about 3 minutes on each side. Serve with dairy sour cream if desired.

Twice-Baked Yams

6 servings

6   medium yams or sweet potatoes
    Vegetable oil
1/4 cup dairy sour cream
1/4 cup milk
2   tablespoons packed brown sugar
2   tablespoons margarine or butter
1/8 teaspoon salt
2   tablespoons coarsely chopped pecans

Rub skins of potatoes with oil; prick with fork to allow steam to escape. Cook in 375° oven until tender, 35 to 45 minutes. Cut thin lengthwise slice from each potato; scoop out inside, leaving a thin shell. Mash potatoes until no lumps remain. Beat in sour cream and milk. Beat in brown sugar, margarine and salt until light and fluffy; stir in pecans.

Place shells in ungreased 13 × 9 × 2-inch baking dish; fill shells with potato mixture. Top each with pecan half if desired. (To serve immediately, cook uncovered in 400° oven until filling is golden, about 20 minutes.) Cover and refrigerate no longer than 24 hours.

TO SERVE: About 30 minutes before serving, heat Twice-Baked Yams uncovered in 400° oven until filling is golden, about 25 minutes.

Left to right: Potato Puffs, Mexican Hash Browns, Potato-Almond Patties, and Twice-Baked Yams

Broiled Squash Kabobs

6 servings

2   *medium zucchini, cut into 1-inch pieces*
2   *medium yellow squash, cut into 1-inch pieces*
12 *cherry tomatoes*
1   *can (16 ounces) small whole onions, drained*
6   *pitted large ripe olives*
¼   *cup vegetable oil*
2   *tablespoons lemon juice*
1   *teaspoon salt*
½   *teaspoon garlic powder*
½   *teaspoon dill weed*

Place vegetables in 13 × 9 × 2-inch baking dish. Mix remaining ingredients; pour over vegetables. Cover and refrigerate at least 8 hours but no longer than 24 hours.

TO SERVE: About 20 minutes before serving, remove vegetables, reserving marinade. Alternate zucchini, yellow squash, tomatoes, onions and olives on six 12-inch metal skewers. Place kabobs crosswise on ungreased 15½ × 10½ × 1-inch jelly roll pan; brush with marinade. Set oven control to broil and/or 550°. Broil with tops 3 to 4 inches from heat until light brown, about 7 minutes. Turn; brush with marinade. Broil until squash is tender, about 5 minutes longer.

VEGETABLE FREEZER TIPS

Keep chopped onion in your freezer to eliminate last minute chopping. Place peeled, chopped onion in boiling water about 1½ minutes. Chill immediately in ice water. Drain, package and freeze. Stir frozen onion into mixtures at the beginning of the cooking time or thaw at room temperature.

Freeze small amounts of leftovers such as crumbled fried bacon, water chestnuts, shredded cheese, toasted chopped nuts and buttered bread crumbs. Stir in or sprinkle one or more on top of hot cooked vegetables.

Rice-Stuffed Tomatoes

6 servings

½   *cup water*
1   *tablespoon instant chicken bouillon*
1   *teaspoon instant minced onion*
2   *slices (¾ ounce each) process American cheese*
½   *cup uncooked instant rice*
1   *teaspoon parsley flakes*
6   *medium tomatoes*

Heat water, bouillon and onion to boiling in 1-quart saucepan. Stir in cheese until smooth. Stir in rice and parsley; remove from heat. Cover and let stand 10 minutes.

Remove stem ends from tomatoes; cut thin slice from bottom of each tomato to prevent tipping. Remove pulp from each tomato, leaving a ¼-inch wall. Chop enough pulp to measure ¼ cup; stir into rice.

Place tomatoes in ungreased 12 × 7½ × 2-inch baking dish. Fill tomatoes with rice mixture. (To serve immediately, cook uncovered in 350° oven until tomatoes are hot, about 20 minutes. Sprinkle with crisply fried and crumbled bacon if desired.) Cover and refrigerate no longer than 24 hours.

TO SERVE: About 30 minutes before serving, cook Rice-Stuffed Tomatoes uncovered in 350° oven until tomatoes are hot, 20 to 25 minutes. Sprinkle with crisply fried and crumbled bacon if desired.

■ *Microwave Directions:* Mix water, bouillon and onion in 1-quart microwaveproof casserole. Cover tightly and microwave on high (100%) until boiling, 2 to 3 minutes. Continue as directed except — arrange tomatoes in circle in ungreased 9- or 10-inch pie plate; fill with rice mixture. Cover loosely and microwave 2 minutes. Rotate dish ½ turn. Microwave until tomatoes and rice mixture are hot, 1 to 3 minutes longer.

Stuffed Zucchini

6 servings

3   medium zucchini (about 1½ pounds)
1   medium onion, chopped (about ½ cup)
¼   cup margarine or butter
1   small green pepper, chopped (about ½ cup)
1   jar (2 ounces) diced pimiento, drained
1   cup herb-seasoned stuffing mix
½   cup shredded mozzarella cheese

Heat 2 inches salted water (½ teaspoon salt to 1 cup water) to boiling. Add zucchini. Cover and heat to boiling. Cook just until tender, 8 to 10 minutes; drain. Cool slightly; cut each zucchini lengthwise into halves. Spoon out pulp; chop coarsely. Place zucchini, cut sides up, in ungreased 11 × 7 × 1½-inch baking pan.

Cook and stir onion in margarine in 10-inch skillet until tender. Stir in chopped pulp, green pepper, pimiento and stuffing mix. Divide stuffing mixture among zucchini halves. Sprinkle each with about 1 tablespoon cheese. (To serve immediately, cook uncovered in 350° oven until hot and cheese is melted, 25 to 30 minutes.) Cover and refrigerate no longer than 24 hours.

TO SERVE: About 40 minutes before serving, cook Stuffed Zucchini uncovered in 350° oven until hot, 30 to 35 minutes.

Microwave Directions: Place zucchini in ungreased microwaveproof platter or 11 × 7 × 1½-inch dish. Cover tightly and microwave on high (100%) 3 minutes; turn zucchini over and rearrange. Cover and microwave just until tender, 2 to 4 minutes longer. Cool slightly; finish preparing zucchini as directed above. Place onion and margarine in 1½-quart microwaveproof casserole. Microwave uncovered, stirring every minute, until tender, 2 to 3 minutes. Stir in chopped pulp, green pepper, pimiento and stuffing mix. Divide stuffing mixture among zucchini halves. Cover loosely and microwave 3 minutes. Rotate dish ½ turn. Microwave until hot, 2 to 4 minutes longer. Sprinkle each half with about 1 tablespoon cheese. Cover and let stand 3 minutes.

Stuffed Zucchini

Macaroni and Vegetables

6 servings

1   cup uncooked spiral or elbow macaroni
        (about 4 ounces)
1   medium zucchini, cut into ³/₈-inch slices
1   medium tomato, coarsely chopped (about 1 cup)
1   medium onion, chopped (about ½ cup)
1   small green pepper, chopped (about ½ cup)
1   large clove garlic, finely chopped
2   tablespoons olive oil or vegetable oil
1   teaspoon salt
¼   teaspoon dried basil leaves
⅛   teaspoon pepper

Cook macaroni as directed on package; drain. Cook and stir zucchini, tomato, onion, green pepper and garlic in oil in 10-inch skillet over medium heat 3 minutes. Stir in macaroni and the remaining ingredients. Cook, stirring occasionally, until zucchini is crisp-tender, about 3 minutes. Serve with grated Parmesan cheese if desired.

Dilled Ziti

6 to 8 servings

3   cups uncooked ziti macaroni
¾   cup mayonnaise or salad dressing
1   tablespoon lemon juice
½   teaspoon salt
¼   teaspoon garlic powder
¼   teaspoon dried dill weed
2   green onions (with tops), thinly sliced

Cook macaroni as directed on package; drain. Stir in mayonnaise, lemon juice, salt, garlic powder and dill weed. Heat, stirring constantly, just until sauce is hot. Sprinkle with onions.

Mexican-Style Macaroni

6 servings

3   cups uncooked macaroni shells
        (about 12 ounces)
1   can (4 ounces) chopped green chilies, drained
1   jar (2 ounces) diced pimiento, drained
1   cup half-and-half
½   cup shredded Cheddar cheese
½   cup sliced ripe olives
½   teaspoon salt

Cook macaroni as directed on package; drain. Stir in remaining ingredients. Cook over low heat, stirring occasionally, until cheese is melted and sauce is hot, about 5 minutes.

Spaghetti with Capers

8 servings

1   package (7 ounces) spaghetti
2   cloves garlic, crushed
½   cup margarine or butter
½   cup dry white wine or apple juice
2   tablespoons capers
1   tablespoon lemon juice
1   teaspoon dried basil leaves
½   teaspoon salt
½   teaspoon freshly ground pepper
2   tablespoons snipped parsley

Cook spaghetti as directed on package; drain. Cook garlic in margarine in 1-quart saucepan over medium heat until garlic is golden brown; remove garlic and discard. Stir in wine, capers, lemon juice, basil, salt and pepper. Heat just until hot; pour over spaghetti. Toss until spaghetti is coated with caper mixture; sprinkle with parsley.

Macaroni and Vegetables

Creole Noodles

6 servings

8 ounces uncooked wide egg noodles
1 medium onion, chopped (about ½ cup)
1 small green pepper, chopped (about ½ cup)
2 tablespoons margarine or butter
1 carton (6 ounces) plain yogurt
½ cup chili sauce
1 teaspoon dry mustard

Cook noodles as directed on package; drain. Cook and stir onion and green pepper in margarine in 2-quart saucepan over medium heat until tender. Stir in yogurt, chili sauce and mustard. Heat, stirring constantly, just until hot. Add noodles; toss until coated with yogurt mixture. Sprinkle with snipped parsley if desired.

Bulgur Pilaf

6 to 8 servings

1 cup uncooked bulgur wheat
1 medium onion, chopped (about ½ cup)
1 medium stalk celery, sliced (about ½ cup)
2 tablespoons margarine or butter
1 can (10½ ounces) condensed beef broth
1 can (4 ounces) mushroom stems and
   pieces, drained
⅔ cup water
½ teaspoon salt
⅛ teaspoon pepper
¼ cup sliced almonds

Cook wheat, onion and celery in margarine in 2-quart saucepan over medium heat, stirring frequently, until onion is tender and wheat is brown, about 5 minutes. Stir in broth, mushrooms, water, salt and pepper. Heat to boiling; reduce heat. Cover and simmer until liquid is absorbed, 15 to 17 minutes. Stir in almonds.

Rice and Avocado

6 servings

Cook 1 package (6 ounces) long grain and wild rice mix as directed on package. Stir in ½ cup sliced ripe olives and 1 large avocado, cut into 1-inch pieces.

Quick Hopping John

6 servings

1⅓ cups water
⅓ cup chopped onion
¾ teaspoon salt
¼ to ½ teaspoon red pepper sauce
1⅓ cups uncooked instant rice
1 can (15 ounces) black-eyed peas, drained
3 slices bacon, crisply fried and crumbled

Heat water, onion, salt and pepper sauce to boiling in 2-quart saucepan. Stir in rice; remove from heat. Cover and let stand until liquid is absorbed, about 10 minutes. Stir in peas and bacon.

Rice with Nuts and Raisins

6 servings

1 cup uncooked regular rice
1 medium onion, chopped (about ½ cup)
2 tablespoons margarine or butter
1 can (10¾ ounces) condensed chicken broth
⅔ cup water
¼ cup raisins
¼ teaspoon salt
⅛ teaspoon pepper
1 jar (1 ounce) pine nuts

Cook and stir rice and onion in margarine in 2-quart saucepan over medium-high heat until rice is light brown. Stir in broth, water, raisins, salt and pepper. Heat to boiling; reduce heat. Cover and simmer 14 minutes. (Do not lift cover or stir.) Remove from heat; stir in pine nuts. Cover and let steam 5 to 10 minutes.

Cheese-Grits Casserole

Cheese-Grits Casserole

8 servings

4 cups water
1 teaspoon salt
1 cup quick-cooking hominy grits
1 cup shredded Cheddar cheese (about 4 ounces)
¼ cup margarine or butter
2 eggs, slightly beaten

Heat water and salt to boiling in 3-quart saucepan. Gradually stir in grits. Heat to boiling; reduce heat. Simmer uncovered, stirring occasionally, 5 minutes; remove from heat. Stir in cheese, margarine and eggs. Pour into ungreased 1½-quart casserole. (To serve immediately, cook uncovered in 350° oven until light golden brown, about 50 minutes.) Cover and refrigerate no longer than 24 hours.

TO SERVE: About 55 minutes before serving, cook Cheese-Grits Casserole uncovered in 350° oven until top is firm and cracks are dry, about 50 minutes.

Baked Parmesan Squares

8 servings

3¾ cups milk
1½ cups cornmeal
3 eggs, well beaten
½ cup grated Parmesan cheese
½ teaspoon salt
¼ cup margarine or butter
½ cup grated Parmesan cheese

Heat milk to scalding in 3-quart saucepan; reduce heat. Gradually stir in cornmeal. Cook, stirring constantly, until thick, about 5 minutes; remove from heat. Mix in eggs, ½ cup cheese and the salt; beat until smooth. Spread in greased 12 × 7½ × 2-inch baking dish. Drizzle with margarine; sprinkle with ½ cup cheese. (To serve immediately, cook uncovered in 425° oven until golden brown, 30 to 35 minutes.) Cover and refrigerate no longer than 24 hours.

TO SERVE: About 45 minutes before serving, cook Baked Parmesan Squares uncovered in 425° oven until golden, 35 to 40 minutes.

Cheese Twists

6 twists

2 tablespoons finely chopped green onions
     (with tops)
2 tablespoons shredded Cheddar cheese
1 tablespoon margarine or butter, softened
½ cup buttermilk baking mix
2 tablespoons milk
    Margarine or butter, softened
    Salt

Heat oven to 425°. Mix onions, cheese and 1 tablespoon margarine. Mix baking mix and milk until soft dough forms. Smooth dough into ball on lightly floured cloth-covered board; knead 5 times. Roll or pat into rectangle, 8×6 inches.

Spread onion mixture over rectangle to within 2 inches of one 8-inch side. Beginning with plain side, fold rectangle lengthwise into thirds; flatten to 2¾ inches in width. Cut crosswise into 6 strips. Twist each strip twice. Place on ungreased cookie sheet; press ends on sheet to fasten securely. Brush with margarine; sprinkle with salt. Bake until light brown, about 10 minutes. Serve warm.

Golden Breadsticks

8 sticks

⅓ cup margarine or butter
1½ cups buttermilk baking mix
⅓ cup milk
    Salt

Heat oven to 450°. Heat margarine in 13×9×2-inch baking pan in oven until melted. Mix baking mix and milk until soft dough forms. Smooth dough into ball on floured cloth-covered board; knead 5 times. Roll into rectangle, 6×4 inches. Cut lengthwise into 8 strips. Dip each strip into melted margarine, coating all sides; arrange in pan. Sprinkle with salt. Bake until golden brown, 10 to 12 minutes.

Seasoned French Bread

1 dozen slices

Cut 1-pound loaf French bread crosswise into halves; reserve one half for future use. Cut remaining half diagonally into 1-inch slices. Spread 1 side of each slice with 1 of the spreads (below). Reassemble slices into loaf; wrap securely in aluminum foil. Heat in 350° oven until warm, about 15 minutes.

Herb Spread

⅓ cup margarine or butter, softened
2 tablespoons grated Parmesan cheese
¼ teaspoon dried basil leaves
¼ teaspoon dried oregano leaves

Mix all ingredients.

Onion Spread

⅓ cup margarine or butter, softened
2 tablespoons finely chopped onion
    Dash of cayenne pepper

Mix all ingredients.

Blue Cheese Spread

⅓ cup margarine or butter, softened
¼ cup finely crumbled blue cheese
¼ teaspoon garlic powder

Mix all ingredients.

Garlic Spread

Mix ⅓ cup margarine or butter, softened and ¼ teaspoon garlic powder.

Toasted Breadsticks

16 sticks

Spread 4 slices bread with margarine or butter, softened; sprinkle with garlic salt, sesame seed, Italian seasoning or grated Parmesan cheese. Cut each slice into 4 strips; place on ungreased cookie sheet. Heat in 350° oven until crisp and golden, 15 to 18 minutes.

Parmesan Bread

8 wedges

1½ cups buttermilk baking mix
1   egg
¼   cup sliced green onions (with tops)
¼   cup milk
¼   cup dry white wine or apple juice
1   tablespoon sugar
½   teaspoon dried tarragon leaves
¼   cup grated Parmesan cheese

Heat oven to 400°. Grease 8 × 1½-inch round baking pan. Mix all ingredients except cheese; beat vigorously 30 seconds. Spread in pan; sprinkle with cheese. Bake until golden brown, 20 to 25 minutes. Cut into wedges; serve immediately.

Seeded Rolls

1 dozen rolls

1   package (8 ounces) brown-and-serve rolls
2   tablespoons margarine or butter, melted
¼   teaspoon onion salt
½   teaspoon sesame seed, poppy seed, caraway seed
      or celery seed

Place rolls on ungreased cookie sheet; brush tops with margarine. Sprinkle with onion salt and sesame seed. Bake as directed on package.

Green Chili Italian Bread

1 dozen slices

1   jar (8 ounces) pasteurized process cheese spread
1   can (4 ounces) chopped green chilies, drained
1   loaf (1 pound) Italian bread

Mix cheese spread and chilies. Cut loaf diagonally into 1-inch slices to within ½ inch of bottom. Spread both sides of each slice with cheese mixture. Place loaf on 18 × 8-inch piece of aluminum foil. Bring foil up around loaf, pressing against sides and leaving top uncovered. Heat in 350° oven until hot and crusty, about 20 minutes.

Cheese and Dill Muffins

Cheese and Dill Muffins

1 dozen muffins

2   cups buttermilk baking mix
⅔   cup milk
½   cup shredded process sharp American cheese
¼   teaspoon dried dill weed

Heat oven to 450°. Grease twelve 2½ × 1¼-inch muffin cups. Mix all ingredients until soft dough forms. Drop dough by spoonfuls into muffin cups. Bake until muffins are light brown, 10 to 15 minutes.

Basic Baking Mix

About 12 cups mix

10½   cups all-purpose flour
¼   cup plus 1 tablespoon baking powder
1   tablespoon plus 1½ teaspoons salt
2   cups shortening

Mix flour, baking powder and salt in 4-quart bowl. Cut in shortening until mixture resembles fine crumbs. Cover, label and store in airtight container at room temperature no longer than 3 months. Use Basic Baking Mix in Baking Powder Biscuits (below), Muffins (right), Pancakes (page 106), Waffles (page 106) or Granola Bread (page 106).

Baking Powder Biscuits

About 1 dozen biscuits

Heat oven to 450°. Mix 2¼ cups Basic Baking Mix (above) and just enough of about ¾ cup milk so dough leaves side of bowl and rounds up into a ball. (Too much milk makes dough sticky, not enough makes biscuits dry.)

Turn dough onto lightly floured surface. Knead lightly 10 times. Roll ½ inch thick. Cut with floured 2-inch biscuit cutter. Place about 1 inch apart on ungreased cookie sheet. Bake until golden brown, 10 to 12 minutes. Immediately remove from cookie sheet.

CHEESE BISCUITS: Mix in ½ cup shredded sharp Cheddar or process American cheese.

DROP BISCUITS: Increase milk to 1 cup. Drop dough by rounded spoonfuls onto greased cookie sheet.

PEANUT BUTTER BISCUITS: Mix in ⅓ cup crunchy peanut butter.

SOUR CREAM-CHIVE BISCUITS: Decrease milk to 1 tablespoon. Stir in 1 cup dairy sour cream and 2 tablespoons snipped chives.

SWISS-DILL BISCUITS: Mix in ½ cup shredded Swiss cheese and 1 teaspoon dried dill weed.

Muffins

1 dozen muffins

2   cups Basic Baking Mix (left)
⅔   cup milk
¼   cup sugar
1   egg
2   tablespoons margarine or butter, melted

Heat oven to 400°. Grease bottoms only of twelve 2½ × 1¼-inch muffin cups or line with paper baking cups. Mix all ingredients; beat vigorously 30 seconds. Fill muffin cups about ⅔ full. Bake until golden brown, about 15 minutes. Immediately remove from pan.

AMBROSIA MUFFINS: Stir in 1 can (8¼ ounces) crushed pineapple, drained, ½ cup flaked or shredded coconut and 1 teaspoon grated orange peel.

BACON-HERB MUFFINS: Decrease sugar to 1 tablespoon. Stir in 4 slices bacon, crisply fried and crumbled, 1 tablespoon parsley flakes and ¼ teaspoon Italian seasoning.

CHERRY MUFFINS: Decrease milk to ⅓ cup. Stir in ⅓ cup maraschino cherry juice and ¼ cup chopped maraschino cherries. Mix 2 tablespoons sugar, ¼ teaspoon ground cinnamon and ⅛ teaspoon ground nutmeg; sprinkle over muffins before baking.

CINNAMON MUFFINS: Immediately roll hot muffins in ½ cup margarine or butter, melted, then in mixture of ½ cup sugar and 1 teaspoon ground cinnamon.

OATMEAL-RAISIN MUFFINS: Stir in ¾ cup quick-cooking oats, ½ cup raisins and ½ teaspoon ground allspice.

PRUNE-NUT MUFFINS: Stir in ½ cup cut-up prunes and ½ cup chopped nuts.

Basic Baking Mix, Bacon-Praline Waffles, Oatmeal-Raisin Muffins, Cheese Biscuits, and Apricot-Apple Pancakes

Granola Bread

1 loaf

2 cups Basic Baking Mix (page 105) or
  2¼ cups buttermilk baking mix
1½ cups Granola or Fruited Granola (page 142)
1 cup milk
½ cup sugar
1 egg

Heat oven to 350°. Grease loaf pan, 9 × 5 × 3 inches. Mix all ingredients; beat vigorously 30 seconds. Pour into pan. Bake until wooden pick inserted in center comes out clean, 55 to 60 minutes. Cool slightly; remove from pan. Cool completely before slicing. Serve with cream cheese or whipped butter if desired.

Pancakes

About thirteen 4-inch pancakes

2 cups Basic Baking Mix (page 105)
1½ cups milk
1 egg
1 tablespoon sugar

Beat all ingredients with hand beater until smooth. Grease heated griddle if necessary. (To test griddle, sprinkle with few drops water. If bubbles skitter, heat is just right.)

For each pancake, pour scant ¼ cup batter onto hot griddle. Cook until pancakes are dry around edges. Turn; cook other sides until golden brown. (To keep pancakes hot, stack on hot plate with paper towels in between.)

APRICOT-APPLE PANCAKES: Stir in ¼ cup each cut-up dried apricots and dried apples.

BANANA PANCAKES: Stir in 1 cup mashed banana (about 1 large) and ¼ teaspoon ground nutmeg.

COCONUT-ORANGE PANCAKES: Decrease milk to 1¼ cups. Stir in ½ cup flaked or shredded coconut, 1 teaspoon grated orange peel and ½ cup orange juice.

HAM PANCAKES: Stir in ½ cup cut-up fully cooked smoked ham, 2 tablespoons honey and ⅛ teaspoon ground cloves.

MIXED FRUIT PANCAKES: Stir in 1 can (8¾ ounces) fruit cocktail, drained, and ¼ teaspoon ground ginger.

POTATO PANCAKES: Stir in 1 cup shredded uncooked potato and ¼ cup sliced green onions (with tops).

Waffles

Four 5-inch waffles

2 cups Basic Baking Mix (page 105)
1⅓ cups milk
1 tablespoon sugar
2 tablespoons vegetable oil
1 egg

Heat waffle iron. Beat all ingredients with hand beater until smooth. Pour batter onto center of hot waffle iron. Bake until steaming stops. Remove waffle carefully.

APRICOT WAFFLES: Stir in ⅓ cup apricot jam and 2 teaspoons grated orange peel.

BACON-PRALINE WAFFLES: Decrease milk to 1 cup. Stir in ⅓ cup maple-flavored syrup. Place 2 slices bacon on hot waffle iron. Cover and bake 30 seconds. Lift cover and pour on batter; sprinkle with 2 tablespoons chopped pecans. Continue as directed.

BLUEBERRY WAFFLES: Stir in 1 cup fresh or frozen (thawed and well drained) blueberries.

CHEESE WAFFLES: Stir in 1 cup shredded sharp Cheddar or process American cheese.

POTATO WAFFLES: Stir in 1 cup shredded uncooked potato, well drained, ½ cup shredded Swiss cheese, ¼ cup thinly sliced green onions (with tops) and ½ teaspoon salt.

SUNFLOWER NUT WAFFLES: Stir in ¼ cup salted sunflower nuts.

WHEAT GERM WAFFLES: Sprinkle 1 to 2 teaspoons wheat germ over batter immediately after pouring it onto the iron.

Basic Cornmeal Mix

About 10 cups mix

- 4   cups yellow cornmeal
- 4   cups all-purpose flour
- ¹/₂ cup sugar
- ¹/₄ cup baking powder
- 2   teaspoons salt
- 1   cup shortening

Mix cornmeal, flour, sugar, baking powder and salt in 4-quart bowl. Cut in shortening until mixture resembles fine crumbs. Cover, label and store in airtight container at room temperature no longer than 3 months. Use Basic Cornmeal Mix in Corn Bread (below), Hush Puppies (below right) or Corn Dogs (page 116).

Corn Bread

9 to 12 servings

- 2¹/₃ cups Basic Cornmeal Mix (above)
- 1   cup milk
- 1   egg

Heat oven to 450°. Mix all ingredients (batter will be slightly lumpy). Pour into greased 8×8×2- or 9×9×2-inch baking pan. Bake until golden brown, 20 to 25 minutes.

CORN BREAD LOAF: Grease bottom only of 9×5×3-inch baking pan. Pour batter into pan. Bake 25 to 30 minutes. Cool slightly before slicing.

CORN MUFFINS: Grease bottoms only of twelve 2¹/₂×1¹/₄-inch muffin cups. Fill muffin cups about ⅞ full. Bake about 20 minutes.

CORN STICKS: Grease corn stick pans. Fill pans ²/₃ full. Bake 12 to 15 minutes.

SKILLET CORN BREAD: Pour batter into greased 10-inch ovenproof skillet. Bake about 20 minutes. Serve with maple-flavored syrup if desired.

Skillet Corn Bread, Corn Muffins, Corn Sticks, and Hush Puppies

Hush Puppies

About 3 dozen hush puppies

- Vegetable oil
- 2¹/₂ cups Basic Cornmeal Mix (above left)
- 1¹/₄ cups milk
- 1   egg
- 2   tablespoons finely chopped onion
- ³/₄ teaspoon cayenne pepper

Heat oil (1 inch) to 375°. Mix remaining ingredients. Drop by teaspoonfuls into hot oil. Fry until golden brown, about 2 minutes. Drain on paper towels.

Sandwiches & Soups

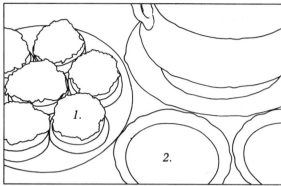

1. Open-Face Chicken Sandwiches, 2. Split Pea Soup

Denver Pocket Sandwiches

6 servings

1 medium onion, chopped (about ½ cup)
1 small green pepper, chopped (about ½ cup)
2 tablespoons margarine or butter
6 eggs
1 can (6¾ ounces) chunk ham or ½ cup
  chopped fully cooked smoked ham
1 jar (2 ounces) diced pimiento, drained
¼ teaspoon salt
⅛ teaspoon pepper
6 large pita breads

Cook and stir onion and green pepper in margarine in 10-inch skillet over medium heat until onion is tender. Beat eggs slightly; stir in ham, pimiento, salt and pepper. Pour egg mixture into skillet. Cook over low heat, gently lifting cooked portions with spatula so that thin uncooked portion can flow to bottom. Avoid constant stirring. Cook until eggs are thickened throughout but still moist, 3 to 5 minutes. Divide among pita breads.

Deli Sandwiches

8 servings

8 frankfurter buns, split
  Prepared mustard
1 pound thinly sliced cooked turkey breast
2 large dill pickles, cut lengthwise into fourths
½ pound thinly sliced fully cooked smoked ham
½ pound sliced Thuringer or salami
1 pint cream-style coleslaw

Spread each bun half with mustard. Layer turkey, pickle, ham and Thuringer on bottom half of each bun. Spoon about ¼ cup coleslaw onto each. Top with remaining bun half.

Ham-Pineapple Sandwiches

4 servings

8 slices whole wheat bread, toasted
  Mayonnaise or salad dressing
1 can (8¼ ounces) crushed pineapple, drained
1 can (6¾ ounces) chunk ham or 4 slices
  fully cooked smoked ham
  Lettuce leaves

Spread toast with mayonnaise. Spread pineapple on 4 slices toast; top with ham and lettuce. Top with remaining slices toast.

TUNA-PINEAPPLE SANDWICHES: Substitute 1 can (6½ ounces) tuna, drained, for the ham. Sprinkle about 1 tablespoon thinly sliced green onion on tuna.

Hoagie Sandwiches

6 servings

1   loaf (1 pound) French bread
     Margarine or butter, softened
4   ounces sliced Swiss cheese
1/2 pound sliced salami
2   cups shredded lettuce
2   medium tomatoes, thinly sliced
1   medium onion, thinly sliced
1/2 pound thinly sliced fully cooked smoked ham
1   medium green pepper, thinly sliced
1/4 cup bottled creamy Italian salad dressing
6   long wooden picks or small skewers

Cut bread horizontally into halves. Spread bottom half with margarine. Layer cheese, salami, lettuce, tomatoes, onion, ham and green pepper on top. Drizzle with dressing; top with remaining half of bread. Secure loaf with picks; cut into 6 pieces.

Heidelberg Sandwiches

6 servings

6   slices rye bread, toasted
     Margarine or butter, softened
     Lettuce leaves
3   medium tomatoes, sliced
1 1/2 pounds braunschweiger, sliced
1   small onion, thinly sliced
1/2 cup mayonnaise or salad dressing
1/3 cup chili sauce
2   tablespoons pickle relish

Spread toast with margarine. Arrange lettuce leaves on toast. Top with tomatoes, braunschweiger and onion. Mix mayonnaise, chili sauce and relish; spoon about 2 tablespoons over top of each.

NOTE: One cup bottled Thousand Island salad dressing can be substituted for the mayonnaise, chili sauce and relish.

Sausage Burritos

6 servings

1   package (12 ounces) bulk seasoned
       pork sausage
1   medium onion, sliced
1   medium green pepper, cut into 1/4-inch strips
6   flour tortillas (10 inches in diameter)
1   can (16 ounces) baked beans in molasses
1/2 head lettuce, shredded (about 3 cups)

Cook and stir pork, onion and green pepper over medium heat until pork is done, about 10 minutes; drain. Prepare tortillas as directed on package. Spoon about 3 tablespoons beans down center of each tortilla. Divide sausage mixture among tortillas. Top with lettuce.

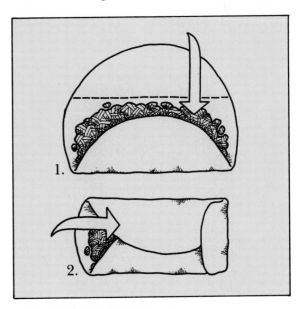

(1) Fold 2 opposite sides of each tortilla over filling. (2) Fold remaining sides over folded sides. Serve with taco sauce if desired.

Quick-Glance Sandwich Chart

Consider the kinds of sandwiches — "open face" with 1 slice of bread or half a roll, "submarine-style" on a split oblong roll, "club" using 3 slices of bread, and the "ordinary sandwich" using 2 slices of bread or a split roll. The chart offers ideas and suggestions for sandwich filling combinations.

FILLINGS	BREADS AND ROLLS	SPREADS AND SAUCES	ADDED INTEREST
Sliced Cooked Meats (Hot or Cold) Beef Chicken Corned Beef Ham Meat Loaf Pastrami Pork Tongue Turkey	Bagels Croissants Kaiser Rolls Onion Rolls Pumpernickel Rye Whole Grain Whole Wheat	Chili Sauce Dairy Sour Cream Horseradish Sauce Mayonnaise or Salad Dressing Mustard Sandwich Spread	Alfalfa Sprouts Avocado Slices Cheese Coleslaw Green Pepper Rings Lettuce Onion Slices Pickle Slices Sauerkraut Spinach Tomato Slices
Eggs Fried Poached Scrambled Sliced Hard-cooked	Bagels English Muffins Onion Rolls Pumpernickel Rye Whole Grain Whole Wheat	Catsup Horseradish Sauce Jelly, Jam or Preserves Mayonnaise or Salad Dressing Mustard Sandwich Spread	Alfalfa Sprouts Avocado Slices Bacon Canadian-style Bacon Green Pepper Rings Lettuce Onion Slices Spinach Tomato Slices
Cheese Cheddar Colby Flavored Cheese Monterey Jack Muenster Process American Cream Cheese Swiss	Bagels English Muffins Nut Breads Pumpernickel Raisin Bread Rye Whole Grain Whole Wheat	Catsup Chili Sauce Mayonnaise or Salad Dressing Mustard	Alfalfa Sprouts Apple Slices Avocado Slices Bacon Canadian-style Bacon Crushed Pineapple Green Pepper Rings Lettuce Onion Slices Sardines Tomato Slices
Salads Chicken Corned Beef Crabmeat Egg Salmon Shrimp Tuna Turkey	Bagels Croissants English Muffins Hard Rolls Pita Bread Tortillas Whole Grain Whole Wheat	Chili Sauce Dairy Sour Cream Horseradish Sauce Mustard Yogurt	Avocado Slices Chopped Apple Chopped Green Pepper Chopped Nuts Chopped Water Chestnuts Crumbled Bacon Cut-up Dried Fruits Olive Slices Tomato Slices

FILLINGS	BREADS AND ROLLS	SPREADS AND SAUCES	ADDED INTEREST
PEANUT BUTTER Creamy Crunchy	Bagels Croissants English Muffins Nut Breads Pumpernickel Raisin Bread Tortillas Whole Grain Whole Wheat	Chili Sauce Honey Jelly, Jam or Preserves Marshmallow Creme	Apple Slices Avocado Slices Bacon Banana Slices Cheese Cut-up Dried Fruits Finely Chopped Onion Raisins

ASSORTED COLD CUTS
Bologna
Liverwurst
Luncheon Loaves
Salami
	Bagels
	Frankfurter Buns
	Individual French
	  Loaves
	Kaiser Rolls
	Onion Rolls
		Blue Cheese Dressing
		Catsup
		Horseradish Sauce
		Mayonnaise or Salad
		  Dressing
		Mustard
		Thousand Island
		  Dressing
			Alfalfa Sprouts
			Avocado Slices
			Cheese
			Coleslaw
			Cucumber Slices
			Onion Slices
			Pickle Slices
			Radish Slices
			Shredded Lettuce
			Tomato Slices

CANNED MEATS
Chunk Chicken
Chunk Ham
Corned Beef
Deviled Ham
Pork Luncheon
  Meat
	English Muffins
	Hamburger Buns
	Onion Rolls
	Pumpernickel
	Raisin Bread
	Rye
	Whole Grain
	Whole Wheat
		Horseradish Sauce
		Mayonnaise or Salad
		  Dressing
		Mustard
		Pickle Relish
		Sandwich Spread
			Alfalfa Sprouts
			Avocado Slices
			Cheese
			Coleslaw
			Green Pepper Rings
			Canned Pineapple Rings
			Lettuce
			Onion Slices
			Spinach
			Tomato Slices

FULLY COOKED SAUSAGES
Bratwurst
Frankfurters
Italian
Knockwurst
Polish
	Frankfurter/Sausage
	  Buns
	Individual French
	  Loaves
	Pumpernickel
	Rye
	Tortillas
		Barbecue Sauce
		Catsup
		Chili Sauce
		Horseradish Sauce
		Mustard
		Pickle Relish
			Alfalfa Sprouts
			Cheese
			Coleslaw
			Shredded Lettuce
			Onion Slices
			Sauerkraut
			Tomato Slices

HAMBURGER PATTIES	Bagels English Muffins French Bread Hamburger Buns Kaiser Rolls Pumpernickel Rye Whole Grain Whole Wheat	Barbecue Sauce Blue Cheese Dressing Catsup Chili Sauce Horseradish Sauce Mayonnaise or Salad Dressing Mustard Peanut Butter Pickle Relish	Alfalfa Sprouts Bacon Canned Pineapple Rings Cheese Coleslaw Green Pepper Rings Lettuce Mushroom Slices Onion Slices Tomato Slices

Hot Dog Roll-Ups

8 servings

8   frankfurters
8   slices white sandwich bread
¼   cup mayonnaise or salad dressing
2   tablespoons finely chopped onion
2   tablespoons pickle relish
1   tablespoon prepared mustard
¼   cup margarine or butter, melted

Place frankfurter in center of each slice bread. Mix mayonnaise, onion, relish and mustard. Spoon about 2 teaspoons mayonnaise mixture over each frankfurter. Bring sides of bread up over frankfurter; secure with wooden picks. Place roll-ups, seam sides down, in ungreased 13 × 9 × 2-inch baking dish. Brush with margarine. Cook uncovered in 350° oven until hot and golden brown, about 20 minutes.

Pork Burgers

4 servings

2   tablespoons margarine or butter
1   can (12 ounces) pork luncheon meat,
         cut into 8 slices
1   medium onion, sliced and separated into rings
1   can (4 ounces) mushroom stems and pieces,
         drained
4   hamburger buns, split and toasted
     Mustard
     Lettuce leaves

Heat margarine in 10-inch skillet over medium heat until melted. Cook luncheon meat in margarine until brown; turn. Cook other sides until brown. Remove from skillet; keep warm. Cook onion and mushrooms in same skillet, stirring occasionally, until onion is tender. Spread each bun half with mustard. Place 2 slices meat, the onion mixture and lettuce on bottom half of each bun. Top with remaining bun half.

Broiled Cheese Sandwiches

8 servings

1   cup shredded Cheddar cheese (about 4 ounces)
1   cup shredded Monterey Jack cheese
         (about 4 ounces)
1   medium onion, chopped (about ½ cup)
⅓   cup margarine or butter, softened
8   slices diagonally cut French bread
         (about ¾ inch thick), toasted

Mix Cheddar and Monterey Jack cheeses, onion and margarine. Spread to edges of toast. Set oven control to broil and/or 550°. Broil with tops about 5 inches from heat until cheese is melted and bubbly, about 2 minutes.

BROILED WINE-CHEESE SANDWICHES: Place toast in ungreased 15½ × 10½ × 1-inch jelly roll pan. Drizzle 1 tablespoon dry white wine over each slice toast; spread with cheese mixture. Continue as directed.

Artichoke-Cheese Sandwiches

6 servings

1   can (14 ounces) artichoke hearts, drained
         and cut into fourths
6   slices rye bread, toasted
1   cup mayonnaise or salad dressing
1   cup shredded Swiss cheese (about 4 ounces)
3   slices bacon, crisply fried and crumbled, or
         2 tablespoons imitation bacon bits

Arrange artichokes on toast. Mix mayonnaise, cheese and bacon; spread over artichokes to edges of toast. Set oven control to broil and/or 550°. Broil with tops about 5 inches from heat until cheese is melted and bubbly, about 2 minutes. Cut each sandwich into thirds. Garnish with cherry tomatoes and pitted ripe olives if desired.

Shrimp Club Sandwiches

Shrimp Club Sandwiches

4 servings

12   slices bacon
     Mayonnaise or salad dressing
12   slices white bread, toasted
 4   lettuce leaves
12   slices tomatoes (about 2 medium)
 2   cans (4½ ounces each) large shrimp,
     rinsed and drained
 1   large avocado, thinly sliced

Fry bacon until crisp; drain. Spread mayonnaise over 1 side of each slice toast. Place lettuce leaf, 3 slices tomato and 3 slices bacon on each of 4 slices toast. Top with another slice toast. Arrange shrimp on toast; top with avocado slices. Top with third slice toast; secure with wooden picks. Cut sandwiches diagonally into 4 triangles.

TURKEY CLUB SANDWICHES: Substitute 4 slices cooked turkey or chicken for the shrimp.

Open-Face Chicken Sandwiches

6 servings

2   cans (5 ounces each) chunk chicken, drained
½   cup mayonnaise or salad dressing
2   stalks celery, chopped (about ½ cup)
¼   cup chopped toasted almonds
½   teaspoon onion salt
2   medium tomatoes, thinly sliced
3   whole wheat English muffins, split and toasted
1   container (6 ounces) frozen avocado dip,
     thawed

Mix chicken, mayonnaise, celery, almonds and onion salt. Arrange tomato slices on each muffin half. Spoon chicken mixture onto tomatoes. Spoon avocado dip onto chicken mixture. Sprinkle with sliced green onions or snipped parsley if desired.

Corn Dogs

5 servings

1   pound frankfurters
      Vegetable oil
1   cup Basic Cornmeal Mix (page 107)
½   cup milk
1   egg

Pat frankfurters dry with paper towels. Heat oil (2 inches) to 365°. Mix cornmeal mix, milk and egg. Dip frankfurters into batter, allowing excess batter to drip into bowl. Fry, turning once, until golden brown, about 4 minutes; drain on paper towels. Insert wooden skewer in end of each frankfurter if desired.

Hot Vegetable Sandwiches

6 servings

6   unsliced whole wheat or
        white hamburger buns
1½   cups shredded Swiss cheese (about 6 ounces)
¼   cup mayonnaise or salad dressing
½   teaspoon salt
½   teaspoon dried basil leaves
2   small zucchini, thinly sliced (about 1 cup)
1   large tomato, chopped (about 1 cup)
1   medium onion, chopped (about ½ cup)
1   can (2 ounces) sliced ripe olives, drained

Cut thin slice from top of each bun; reserve. Remove center from each bun, leaving ¼-inch wall. (Use removed bread for bread crumbs or stuffing.) Mix cheese, mayonnaise, salt and basil; spread about ¼ cup in bottom of each bun. Mix zucchini, tomato, onion and olives; divide among buns. Top with reserved tops of buns. Wrap each sandwich in heavy-duty aluminum foil. (To serve immediately, heat on oven rack in 350° oven until hot and cheese is melted, about 25 minutes.) Refrigerate no longer than 24 hours.

TO SERVE: About 35 minutes before serving, heat wrapped Hot Vegetable Sandwiches on oven rack in 350° oven until hot and cheese is melted, about 30 minutes.

Hot Vegetable Sandwiches

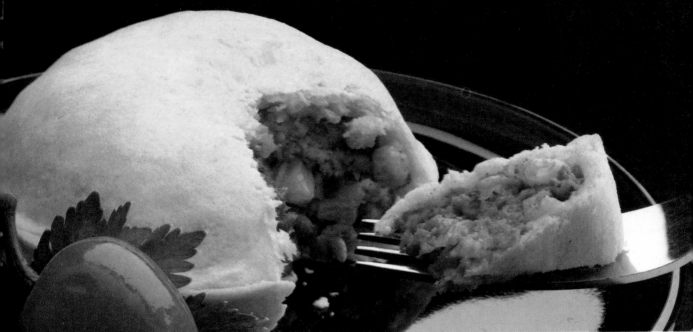

Chiliburgers in Crusts

Chiliburgers in Crusts

6 servings

1½ pounds ground beef
1 can (8 ounces) whole kernel corn, drained
1 can (4 ounces) chopped green chilies, drained
2 teaspoons chili powder
1 teaspoon salt
2⅓ cups buttermilk baking mix
3 tablespoons margarine or butter, melted
½ cup milk

Mix ground beef, corn, chilies, chili powder and salt. Shape mixture into 6 patties; place on rack in broiler pan. Set oven control to broil and/or 550°. Broil with tops 3 to 4 inches from heat 4 minutes on each side. Mix remaining ingredients until soft dough forms; beat vigorously 20 strokes. Gently smooth dough into ball on floured cloth-covered board. Knead 5 times. Roll ⅛ inch thick. Cut with floured 4½-inch biscuit cutter. Place beef patties on 6 of the rounds; top each with another round. Pinch edges together to seal. (To serve immediately, place on ungreased cookie sheet. Bake in 400° oven until golden brown, about 15 minutes.) Cover and refrigerate no longer than 24 hours.

TO SERVE: About 25 minutes before serving, place chiliburgers on ungreased cookie sheet. Bake in 400° oven until beef is hot and crust is golden brown, about 20 minutes.

Continental Beef Au Jus

6 servings

1½ - pound beef boneless round steak (¾ inch thick)
3 tablespoons soy sauce
1 tablespoon vegetable oil
1 tablespoon catsup
½ teaspoon salt
½ teaspoon ground ginger
½ teaspoon dried oregano leaves
1 clove garlic, finely chopped

Have ready at serving time:

1 package (1 ounce) au jus mix
6 kaiser or onion rolls, split and buttered

Place beef on large piece of plastic wrap. Mix soy sauce, oil, catsup, salt, ginger, oregano and garlic; brush over both sides of beef. Fold plastic wrap over beef and seal securely. Refrigerate beef at least 5 hours but no longer than 24 hours.

TO SERVE: About 20 minutes before serving, unwrap beef and place on rack in broiler pan. Set oven control to broil and/or 550°. Broil beef with top about 3 inches from heat until medium doneness, 7 to 8 minutes on each side. Prepare au jus mix as directed on package; stir in beef juices from the broiler pan. Cut beef into thin slices; fill rolls with beef. Serve sandwiches with juice.

Piroshki

4 servings

1 pound ground beef
1 medium onion, chopped (about ½ cup)
½ cup shredded Cheddar cheese
½ teaspoon salt
⅛ teaspoon pepper
2 cups buttermilk baking mix
½ cup cold water
 Margarine or butter, melted

Have ready at serving time:

Chili sauce or catsup

Cook and stir ground beef and onion until brown; drain. Stir in cheese, salt and pepper. Mix baking mix and cold water until soft dough forms; beat vigorously 20 strokes. Gently smooth dough into ball on floured cloth-covered board. Knead 5 times. Roll dough into 16-inch square; cut into 4 squares.

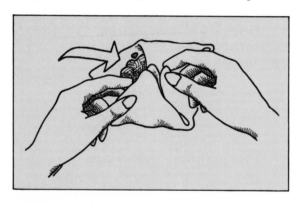

Place 1 cup beef mixture in center of each square. Bring opposite corners together at center to form triangles. Pinch edges together to seal securely, making 4 diagonal seams. Brush with margarine. (To serve immediately, place on ungreased cookie sheet. Bake in 450° oven until golden brown, about 10 minutes. Serve with chili sauce.) Cover and refrigerate no longer than 24 hours.

TO SERVE: About 20 minutes before serving, place Piroshki on ungreased cookie sheet. Bake in 450° oven until beef mixture is hot and crust is golden brown, about 15 minutes. Serve with chili sauce.

Sloppy Joes

3 meals - 5 servings each

3 pounds ground beef
2 large onions, chopped (about 2 cups)
4 medium stalks celery, sliced (about 2 cups)
2 cloves garlic, finely chopped
1½ cups catsup
¾ cup water
2 tablespoons Worcestershire sauce
2½ teaspoons salt
½ teaspoon pepper

Have ready at serving time for each meal:

5 hamburger buns, split and toasted

Cook and stir ground beef, onions, celery and garlic in 4-quart Dutch oven until beef is light brown; drain. Stir in catsup, water, Worcestershire sauce, salt and pepper. Heat to boiling; reduce heat. Cover and simmer, stirring occasionally, 15 minutes. (To serve immediately, remove ⅓ of the beef mixture [about 1¾ cups] and fill buns.) Divide beef mixture among three 1-pint freezer containers. Cover, label and freeze no longer than 3 months.

TO SERVE: About 35 minutes before serving, remove 1 container beef mixture from freezer. Dip into very hot water just to loosen. Place frozen block in 2-quart saucepan. Heat uncovered over medium heat, turning occasionally, until hot, about 30 minutes. Fill buns with beef mixture.

■ *Microwave Reheat Directions:* Dip 1 container beef mixture into very hot water just to loosen. Place frozen block in 2-quart microwaveproof casserole. Cover tightly and microwave on high (100%), stirring every 5 minutes, until hot, 14 to 16 minutes.

CHILI SLOPPY JOES: Heat 1 container beef mixture as directed. Stir in 1 can (4 ounces) chopped green chilies, drained, and 1 teaspoon chili powder.

Hot Beef Sandwiches

2 meals - 6 servings each

4 - pound beef tip, heel of round or rolled
     rump roast
2   tablespoons vegetable oil
2   cans (10½ ounces each) condensed beef broth
2   cups water
1   medium onion, cut into fourths
2   cloves garlic, crushed
1   teaspoon pepper
¾   cup cold water
⅓   cup all-purpose flour

Have ready at serving time for each meal:

¼   cup water
6   hamburger buns, split

Cook beef in oil in 4-quart Dutch oven over medium heat until brown. Add broth, 2 cups water, the onion, garlic and pepper. Heat to boiling; reduce heat. Cover and simmer until beef is tender, about 3 hours.

Remove beef from broth; cool slightly. Shred beef into small pieces with 2 forks. Strain broth; add enough water to measure 4 cups. Return broth mixture to Dutch oven. Skim excess fat. Heat to boiling. Shake ¾ cup cold water and the flour in tightly covered container; gradually stir into broth. Heat to boiling, stirring constantly. Boil and stir 1 minute. Stir in shredded beef. (To serve immediately, remove ½ of the beef mixture [about 3½ cups] and fill buns.) Divide beef mixture between two 1½-quart freezer containers. Cover, label and freeze no longer than 2 months.

TO SERVE: About 40 minutes before serving, remove 1 container beef mixture from freezer. Dip container into very hot water just to loosen. Heat frozen block and ¼ cup water uncovered in 2-quart saucepan over medium heat, turning occasionally, until hot, about 35 minutes. Fill buns with beef mixture.

■ *Microwave Reheat Directions:* Dip 1 container beef mixture into very hot water just to loosen. Place frozen block in 2-quart microwaveproof casserole. Cover tightly and microwave on high (100%), stirring every 5 minutes, until hot, 12 to 14 minutes.

Hot Club Sandwiches

8 servings

8   hard rolls
    Margarine or butter, softened
1   pound sliced fully cooked smoked ham
½   pound sliced cooked turkey or chicken
1   cup shredded mozzarella cheese
    (about 4 ounces)
½   cup crumbled blue cheese

Cut rolls horizontally into thirds. Spread each cut surface with margarine. Place ham on bottom sections of rolls; add second sections of rolls. Top with turkey. Mix cheeses; spread over turkey. Top with third sections of rolls. Wrap each sandwich in aluminum foil. (To serve immediately, heat wrapped sandwiches on oven rack in 425° oven until hot, 15 to 20 minutes.) Label sandwiches and freeze no longer than 1 month.

TO SERVE: About 45 minutes before serving, place wrapped Hot Club Sandwiches on oven rack. Heat in 450° oven until sandwiches are hot, 35 to 40 minutes.

LUNCH BOX FREEZER SANDWICHES

Sandwiches are not only easy to carry and eat but also easy to make and freeze ahead. For greater efficiency, set up an assembly line, making two or three week's worth at a time. Set out a variety of breads and rolls and softened margarine or butter. Skip the mayonnaise, sour cream, hard-cooked eggs and lettuce; they don't freeze well and can be packed separately to add at lunchtime. Use a variety of fillings — sliced cooked meats, cold cuts, peanut butter and cheeses, for example.

Spread each slice of bread thinly with margarine all the way to the edge to prevent the filling from making the bread soggy. Add filling, top with second slice of bread; cut, wrap, label and freeze. Each morning, select and pack a frozen sandwich. Add lettuce, crisp vegetable sticks, fruit and a special snack. Not only will the frozen sandwich thaw in about 3 hours at room temperature, but will also help keep your lunch chilled.

French Onion Soup

6 servings - about 1 cup each

3   large onions, sliced
1/4   cup margarine or butter
1   tablespoon all-purpose flour
2   cans (10 1/2 ounces each) condensed beef broth
2   cups water
1   teaspoon Worcestershire sauce
6   slices French bread, toasted
3   cups shredded Monterey Jack or mozzarella
      cheese (about 12 ounces)

Cook onions in margarine in 4-quart Dutch oven over medium heat, stirring occasionally, until onions are tender and just begin to brown. Sprinkle with flour; gradually stir in 1 can of the broth. Heat to boiling, stirring constantly. Stir in remaining broth, the water and Worcestershire sauce. Heat to boiling; reduce heat. Simmer uncovered 5 minutes. Place 1 slice toast in each of 6 heatproof soup bowls or casseroles; pour soup over toast. Sprinkle with cheese. Set oven control to broil and/or 550°. Broil soups with tops 3 to 4 inches from heat until cheese is melted and light brown, about 5 minutes.

■ *Microwave Directions:* Place onions and margarine in 3-quart microwaveproof casserole. Cover tightly and microwave on high (100%) 4 minutes; stir. Cover and microwave until tender, 4 to 5 minutes longer. Stir in flour, broth, water and Worcestershire sauce. Cover and microwave until boiling, 10 to 12 minutes. Place 1 slice toast in each of 6 heatproof soup bowls or casseroles; pour soup over toast. Sprinkle with cheese. Broil as directed above.

French Onion Soup

Mexican-Style Soup

6 servings - about 1 cup each

1   can (10 3/4 ounces) condensed golden
      mushroom soup
1   can (10 3/4 ounces) condensed cream of
      chicken soup
2   cups milk
2/3   cup half-and-half
1   medium avocado, chopped (about 3/4 cup)
1/4   cup sliced ripe olives
1   can (4 ounces) chopped green chilies, drained
1/2   teaspoon salt

Mix soups, milk and half-and-half in 2-quart saucepan. Heat over low heat, stirring occasionally, just until hot. Stir in remaining ingredients; heat just until hot. Sprinkle with shredded cheese if desired.

■ *Microwave Directions:* Mix soups, milk and half-and-half in 2-quart microwaveproof casserole. Cover tightly and microwave on high (100%), stirring every 3 minutes, until hot, 9 to 11 minutes. Stir in remaining ingredients. Cover and microwave until hot, 2 to 3 minutes.

Chunky Potato Soup

4 servings - about 1 cup each

6   slices bacon, cut up
1   large onion, chopped (about 1 cup)
2   medium stalks celery, chopped (about 1 cup)
1   can (16 ounces) whole potatoes, drained
      and coarsely chopped
1   can (10 3/4 ounces) condensed chicken broth
1/2   cup water
1/4   teaspoon dried thyme leaves
1/8   teaspoon pepper
1   cup milk

Fry bacon in 3-quart saucepan until crisp. Remove bacon with slotted spoon; drain on paper towels. Drain fat from pan, reserving 2 tablespoons in pan. Cook and stir onion and celery in fat until celery is tender, about 6 minutes. Stir in potatoes, broth, water, thyme and pepper. Heat to boiling; reduce heat. Cover and simmer 10 minutes. Stir in milk and bacon; heat just until hot.

Cream of Almond Soup

8 servings - about ½ cup each

1   tablespoon margarine or butter
1   tablespoon all-purpose flour
½   teaspoon salt
⅛   teaspoon pepper
1   can (10¾ ounces) condensed chicken broth
2   cups half-and-half
⅓   cup toasted sliced almonds
½   teaspoon grated lemon peel

Heat margarine in 1½-quart saucepan over low heat until melted. Stir in flour, salt and pepper. Cook over low heat, stirring constantly, until smooth and bubbly; remove from heat. Stir in broth. Heat to boiling, stirring constantly. Boil and stir 1 minute; reduce heat. Stir in remaining ingredients; heat just until soup is hot.

Shrimp Bisque

6 servings - about 1 cup each

2   cans (11 ounces each) condensed tomato bisque
2   soup cans water
2   cans (4½ ounces each) broken shrimp, rinsed and drained
2   teaspoons prepared horseradish
2   teaspoons lemon juice
    Dash of cayenne pepper

Heat all ingredients over low heat, stirring occasionally, until hot. Sprinkle with dried dill weed if desired.

▮ *Microwave Directions:* Mix all ingredients in 2-quart microwaveproof casserole. Cover tightly and microwave on high (100%) 5 minutes; stir. Cover and microwave until hot, 5 to 7 minutes longer.

Beef-Vegetable Soup

8 servings - about 1 cup each

1   pound ground beef
2   medium stalks celery, sliced (about 1 cup)
1   large onion, chopped (about 1 cup)
1   can (16 ounces) whole tomatoes
1   can (16 ounces) diced beets
1   can (16 ounces) diced carrots, drained
1   tablespoon instant beef bouillon
2   teaspoons parsley flakes
1   teaspoon salt
½   teaspoon ground nutmeg
1   can (12 ounces) beer
2   cups shredded cabbage

Cook and stir beef, celery and onion in 4-quart Dutch oven until beef is light brown; drain. Stir in tomatoes (with liquid), beets (with liquid), carrots, bouillon, parsley, salt and nutmeg; break up tomatoes with fork. Heat to boiling; reduce heat. Cover and simmer 10 minutes. Stir in beer and cabbage. Heat to boiling; reduce heat. Cover and simmer until cabbage is crisp-tender, about 5 minutes.

Lima Bean Soup

5 servings - about 1 cup each

1   medium stalk celery, sliced (about ½ cup)
1   medium onion, chopped (about ½ cup)
2   tablespoons margarine or butter
1   can (10¾ ounces) condensed chicken broth
1   soup can water
1   package (10 ounces) frozen baby lima beans
1   can (8 ounces) sliced carrots, drained
1   can (6¾ ounces) chunk ham or 1 cup cut-up fully cooked smoked ham

Cook and stir celery and onion in margarine in 3-quart saucepan until onion is tender. Stir in broth, water and beans. Heat to boiling; reduce heat. Cover and simmer until beans are tender, about 5 minutes. Stir in carrots and ham; heat just until hot.

Green Bean Soup

5 servings - about 1 cup each

2 cups water
1 can (10¾ ounces) condensed chicken broth
1 package (10 ounces) frozen cut green beans
1 small onion, thinly sliced
¼ cup uncooked instant rice
1 teaspoon parsley flakes
¼ teaspoon dried savory leaves
1 can (8 ounces) sliced carrots
1 can (6¾ ounces) chunk ham

Heat water, broth, beans, onion, rice, parsley and savory to boiling in 2-quart saucepan, stirring occasionally; reduce heat. Cover and simmer until beans are tender, about 5 minutes. Stir in carrots (with liquid) and ham; heat just until soup is hot.

Sausage Chowder

5 servings - about 1 cup each

1 package (12 ounces) smoked sausage links, cut into ½-inch slices
1 small green pepper, chopped (about ½ cup)
1 small onion, chopped (about ¼ cup)
1 tablespoon margarine or butter
1 can (16½ ounces) cream-style corn
1 can (10¾ ounces) condensed cream of potato soup
⅔ cup milk

Cook and stir sausage, green pepper and onion in margarine in 3-quart saucepan over medium heat until sausage is brown. Stir in remaining ingredients; heat just until hot.

■*Microwave Directions:* Omit milk. Place sausage, green pepper, onion and margarine in 2-quart casserole. Cover tightly and microwave on high (100%) 2 minutes; stir. Cover and microwave until onion is tender, 2 to 3 minutes longer. Stir in corn and soup. Cover and microwave until hot, 6 to 8 minutes.

Italian Vegetable Soup

Italian Vegetable Soup

8 servings - about 1 cup each

1 pound bulk Italian sausage
1 medium onion, sliced
1 can (16 ounces) whole tomatoes
1 can (15 ounces) garbanzo beans, drained
1 can (10½ ounces) condensed beef broth
1½ cups water
2 medium zucchini or yellow summer squash, cut into ¼-inch slices
½ teaspoon dried basil leaves
   Grated Parmesan cheese

Cook and stir sausage and onion in 3-quart saucepan until sausage is light brown; drain. Stir in tomatoes (with liquid), beans, broth, water, zucchini and basil; break up tomatoes with fork. Heat to boiling; reduce heat. Cover and simmer until zucchini is tender, about 5 minutes. Sprinkle with cheese.

Easy Soup Combos

For a new flavor twist to canned soups, try the following combinations. Gradually stir liquid into soup(s) in saucepan. Stir in suggested addition. Heat just to boiling, stirring occasionally.

CONDENSED SOUP 1 CAN EACH	LIQUID	ADDITION	SERVINGS
BEAN WITH BACON (11½ ounces) VEGETABLE (10½ ounces)	2 soup cans water		5 servings (1 cup each)
CHEDDAR CHEESE (11 ounces) SPLIT PEA WITH HAM AND BACON (11½ ounces)	1 soup can water 1 soup can milk		5 servings (1 cup each)
CHEDDAR CHEESE (11 ounces) TOMATO (10¾ ounces)	1 soup can water 1 soup can milk	To serve, top with croutons or popcorn	5 servings (1 cup each)
CHICKEN (10¾ ounces) CHICKEN WITH RICE (10½ ounces)	1 soup can water	½ teaspoon dried marjoram leaves	3 servings (about ¾ cup each)
CHICKEN NOODLE (10¾ ounces) ONION (10½ ounces)	2 soup cans water		5 servings (1 cup each)
CREAM OF CHICKEN (10¾ ounces)	1 soup can water	¼ teaspoon curry powder	3 servings (about ¾ cup each)
SPLIT PEA WITH HAM AND BACON (11½ ounces)	1 soup can water 1 soup can milk	To serve, top each serving with dollop dairy sour cream	5 servings (1 cup each)
TOMATO (10¾ ounces)	1 soup can milk	¼ teaspoon ground cloves	3 servings (about ¾ cup each)
TOMATO (10¾ ounces) BEEF NOODLE (10¾ ounces)	1 soup can water 1 soup can milk		5 servings (1 cup each)
TOMATO (10¾ ounces) CHICKEN GUMBO (10¾ ounces)	1 soup can water 1 soup can milk		5 servings (1 cup each)

French-Style Chicken Soup

French-Style Chicken Soup

8 servings - about 1½ cups each

2½ - to 3-pound broiler-fryer chicken, cut up
  2   tablespoons vegetable oil
  2   large onions, thinly sliced and separated
          into rings
  2   cloves garlic, finely chopped
  1   can (16 ounces) whole tomatoes
  1   can (10¾ ounces) condensed chicken broth
  1   cup water
  1   cup dry white wine or apple juice
  1   tablespoon sugar
  1   teaspoon dried thyme leaves
  1   teaspoon salt
  ¼   teaspoon pepper

Have ready at serving time:

  1   medium green pepper, cut into ¼-inch strips
  8   slices French bread, toasted
      Snipped parsley

Remove skin from chicken pieces. Heat oil in 4-quart Dutch oven. Cook chicken in oil until brown on all sides; remove chicken from pan. Cook and stir onions and garlic in same pan until onion is tender. Return chicken to pan; add tomatoes (with liquid), broth, water, wine, sugar, thyme, salt and pepper; break up tomatoes with fork. Heat to boiling; reduce heat. Cover and simmer until chicken is done, about 1 hour. (To serve immediately, skim excess fat from chicken mixture. Add green pepper. Heat to boiling; reduce heat. Cover and simmer just until green pepper is tender, about 10 minutes. Place a slice of French bread in each serving bowl. Spoon chicken and broth over bread. Sprinkle with parsley.) Cover and refrigerate no longer than 48 hours.

TO SERVE: About 30 minutes before serving, remove excess fat from French-Style Chicken Soup. Heat to boiling; reduce heat. Cover and simmer until chicken is hot. Add green pepper. Heat to boiling; reduce heat. Cover and simmer until green pepper is tender, about 10 minutes. Place a slice of French bread in each serving bowl. Spoon chicken and broth over bread. Sprinkle with parsley.

Chunky Beef-Noodle Soup

6 servings - about 1 cup each

1   pound beef boneless round steak,
       cut into ¾-inch pieces
1   large onion, chopped (about 1 cup)
2   cloves garlic, finely chopped
1   tablespoon vegetable oil
1   can (16 ounces) whole tomatoes
1   can (10½ ounces) condensed beef broth
2   cups water
2   teaspoons chili powder
1½ teaspoons salt
½   teaspoon dried oregano leaves

Have ready at serving time:

2   ounces uncooked egg noodles (about 1 cup)
1   medium green pepper, coarsely chopped
       (about 1 cup)
¼   cup snipped parsley

Cook and stir beef, onion and garlic in oil in 4-quart Dutch oven until beef is brown, about 15 minutes. Stir in tomatoes (with liquid), broth, water, chili powder, salt and oregano; break up tomatoes with fork. Heat to boiling; reduce heat. Cover and simmer until beef is tender, 1½ to 2 hours. (To serve immediately, skim excess fat from beef. Stir in noodles and green pepper. Heat to boiling; reduce heat. Simmer uncovered until noodles are tender, about 10 minutes. Stir in parsley.) Cover and refrigerate no longer than 48 hours.

TO SERVE: About 30 minutes before serving, remove excess fat from Chunky Beef-Noodle Soup. Heat to boiling; reduce heat. Cover and simmer until beef is hot, about 12 minutes. Stir in noodles and green pepper. Heat to boiling; reduce heat. Simmer uncovered until noodles are tender, about 10 minutes. Stir in parsley.

Bean and Sausage Soup

8 servings - about 1¼ cups each

7   cups water
1   pound dried Great Northern or lima beans
       (about 2 cups)
1   can (16 ounces) whole tomatoes
1   large onion, chopped (about 1 cup)
2   cloves garlic, finely chopped
1   teaspoon salt
½   teaspoon pepper

Have ready at serving time:

1   pound kielbasa or Polish sausage, cut
       into ¼-inch slices
2   medium carrots, cut into ¼-inch slices
       (about 1 cup)
2   medium stalks celery, cut into ¼-inch slices
       (about 1 cup)

Heat water and beans to boiling in 4-quart Dutch oven; boil 2 minutes. Remove from heat; cover and let stand 1 hour.

Add tomatoes (with liquid), onion, garlic, salt and pepper. Heat to boiling; reduce heat. Cover and simmer until beans are tender, about 2 hours. (Do not boil or beans will burst.) Skim fat if necessary. (To serve immediately, cook sausage over medium heat until brown; drain. Stir sausage, carrots and celery into bean mixture. Heat to boiling; reduce heat. Cover and simmer until vegetables are tender, about 30 minutes. Stir in milk or water for thinner consistency.) Cover and refrigerate no longer than 3 days.

TO SERVE: About 45 minutes before serving, heat bean mixture to boiling. Cook sausage over medium heat until brown; drain. Stir sausage, carrots and celery into bean mixture. Heat to boiling; reduce heat. Cover and simmer until vegetables are tender, about 30 minutes. Stir in small amount of milk or water for thinner consistency.

Split Pea Soup

8 servings - about 1½ cups each

8   cups water
1   pound dried split peas (about 2¼ cups)
1   large onion, chopped (about 1 cup)
1   cup finely chopped celery
¼   teaspoon pepper
2   pounds ham shanks, ham hocks or ham bone

Have ready at serving time:

3   medium carrots, cut into ¼-inch slices

Heat water and peas to boiling in 4-quart Dutch oven; boil 2 minutes. Remove from heat; cover and let stand 1 hour. Stir in onion, celery and pepper; add ham shanks. Heat to boiling; reduce heat. Cover and simmer until peas are tender, about 1½ hours. Remove ham shanks; remove ham from bone. Trim excess fat from ham; cut ham into ½-inch pieces. Stir into soup. (To serve immediately, continue as directed in TO SERVE.) Cover and refrigerate no longer than 3 days.

TO SERVE: About 45 minutes before serving, heat Split Pea Soup to boiling; reduce heat. Stir in carrots. Cover and simmer until carrots are tender and soup is desired consistency, about 30 minutes.

Cold Vegetable Soup

5 servings - about 1 cup each

3   cups tomato juice
1   small cucumber, coarsely chopped
1   small green pepper, coarsely chopped
1   small onion, coarsely chopped
2   cloves garlic, cut into halves
2   tablespoons lemon juice
½   teaspoon ground cumin

Have ready at serving time:

Accompaniments (seasoned croutons and about ½ cup each chopped cucumber, tomato, green pepper and onion)

Place 1½ cups of the tomato juice, the cucumber, green pepper, onion, garlic, lemon juice and cumin in blender container. Cover and blend on high speed, stopping blender occasionally to scrape sides, until smooth, about 1 minute. Stir into remaining tomato juice. Cover and refrigerate at least 6 hours but no longer than 48 hours.

TO SERVE: Just before serving, stir Cold Vegetable Soup. Serve with Accompaniments.

Appetizers, Beverages & Desserts

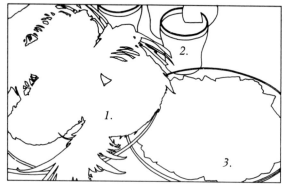

1. *Gingered Pineapple*, 2. *Cranberry Cooler*,
3. *Brie with Almonds*

Avocado Spread

1½ cups spread

2　avocados
½　cup dairy sour cream
1　tablespoon lemon juice
½　teaspoon salt
¼　teaspoon garlic powder
　　Assorted crackers

Mash avocados until smooth; stir in remaining ingredients except crackers. Garnish with snipped parsley or paprika if desired. Serve with crackers.

Chilies Con Queso

About 2⅓ cups dip

1　jar (16 ounces) pasteurized process cheese spread
1　can (4 ounces) chopped green chilies, drained
1　jar (2 ounces) diced pimiento, drained

Heat all ingredients over low heat, stirring constantly, until cheese is melted, about 2 minutes. Pour into fondue pot or chafing dish; keep warm over low heat. Serve with tortilla chips or bite-size fresh vegetables.

Dried Beef Dip

About 2 cups dip

1　cup dairy sour cream
1　cup mayonnaise or salad dressing
1　teaspoon prepared horseradish
¼　teaspoon dried dill weed
1　package (2½ ounces) dried beef, finely chopped

Mix sour cream, mayonnaise, horseradish and dill weed until smooth. Stir in beef. Serve with chips or bite-size fresh vegetables.

SHRIMP DIP: Substitute 1 can (4½ ounces) tiny shrimp, rinsed and drained, for the beef.

Brie with Almonds

8 servings

1　whole round brie cheese (4½ ounces)
2　tablespoons margarine or butter
¼　cup toasted sliced almonds
1　tablespoon brandy, if desired
　　Assorted crackers

Set oven control to broil and/or 550°. Broil cheese with top 3 to 4 inches from heat until soft and warm, about 2½ minutes. Heat margarine until melted; stir in almonds and brandy. Pour over cheese. Garnish with snipped parsley if desired. Serve with crackers.

■ *Microwave Directions:* Microwave cheese uncovered on medium (50%) just until soft and warm, 2 to 3 minutes. Microwave margarine uncovered on high (100%) until melted, about 1 minute. Stir in almonds and brandy; pour over cheese. Garnish with snipped parsley if desired. Serve with crackers.

Parmesan Nuts, and Potato Wedges

Parmesan Nuts

1½ cups nuts

1½   cups whole almonds, pecan halves or
       walnut halves
  2   tablespoons margarine or butter, melted
 ½   teaspoon seasoned salt
 ¼   cup grated Parmesan cheese

Spread almonds in ungreased 13 × 9 × 2-inch baking pan. Cook uncovered in 350° oven, stirring once, until golden brown, about 10 minutes. Mix margarine and seasoned salt; toss with almonds until coated. Sprinkle with cheese. Cook until cheese is light brown, about 4 minutes; stir. Serve warm.

Potato Wedges

4 servings

  2   medium potatoes, each cut into 8 wedges
       Vegetable oil
       Seasoned salt
 ¾   cup dairy sour cream
 ⅓   cup shredded Cheddar cheese

Place potato wedges, cut sides down, on rack in broiler pan. Brush with oil; sprinkle with seasoned salt. Set oven control to broil and/or 550°. Broil with tops about 3 inches from heat until brown, about 5 minutes. Turn; brush with oil. Sprinkle with seasoned salt. Broil until tender, about 5 minutes.

Spoon sour cream onto center of large serving platter; sprinkle with cheese. Arrange potato wedges around sour cream.

Spicy Vegetable Dip

About 1 cup dip

1 cup creamed cottage cheese
2 tablespoons milk
1 tablespoon lemon juice
2 teaspoons Dijon-style mustard
1 teaspoon onion powder
1 teaspoon curry powder

Have ready at serving time:

Assorted vegetable dippers

Place cottage cheese, milk and lemon juice in blender container. Cover and blend on high speed, stopping occasionally to scrape sides, until smooth, about 1 minute. Add mustard, onion powder and curry powder. Cover and blend 1 minute longer. Cover and refrigerate at least 1 hour but no longer than 3 days.

TO SERVE: Just before serving, arrange vegetables on tray or platter with dip.

LOW-CAL SPICY DIP: Substitute 1 carton (8 ounces) plain yogurt for the cottage cheese, milk and lemon juice. Stir mustard, onion powder and curry powder into yogurt.

Swiss-Bacon Appetizers

3 dozen appetizers

8 slices bacon, crisply fried and crumbled
2 cups shredded Swiss cheese (about 8 ounces)
1/3 cup finely chopped onion
1 cup buttermilk baking mix
1 cup half-and-half
4 eggs
1/8 teaspoon cayenne pepper

Sprinkle bacon, cheese and onion in greased 9 × 9 × 2-inch baking pan; cover and refrigerate. Beat remaining ingredients until smooth, 15 seconds in covered blender container on high speed or 1 minute with hand beater. (To serve immediately, continue as directed in TO SERVE.) Cover and refrigerate no longer than 24 hours.

TO SERVE: About 45 minutes before serving, stir egg mixture and pour over onion in pan. Cook uncovered in 375° oven until golden brown and knife inserted in center comes out clean, about 30 minutes. Let stand 10 minutes. Cut into about 1¼-inch squares.

Barbecued Ribs

25 to 30 appetizers

2 - pound rack pork back ribs, cut lengthwise across bones into halves
1/2 cup catsup
2 tablespoons packed brown sugar
1 tablespoon lemon juice
1 teaspoon salt
1/2 teaspoon garlic powder
1/4 teaspoon ground ginger

Have ready at serving time:

3 tablespoons dry mustard
3 tablespoons cold water

Trim excess fat and remove membranes from pork. Mix catsup, brown sugar, lemon juice, salt, garlic powder and ginger; pour over pork, turning to coat both sides. Cover and refrigerate at least 2 hours.

Remove pork; reserve marinade. Place pork on rack in foil-lined broiler pan. Cook uncovered in 400° oven, brushing occasionally with reserved marinade, 30 minutes. Turn pork; cook, brushing occasionally with marinade, until done, about 30 minutes. (Can be served immediately. Mix mustard and water until smooth; serve with pork.) Refrigerate until cool. Wrap, label and freeze no longer than 2 months.

TO SERVE: About 45 minutes before serving, remove Barbecued Ribs from freezer and unwrap. Place in single layer in ungreased 15½ × 10½ × 1-inch jelly roll pan. Cover and heat in 350° oven 20 minutes. Uncover and heat until hot, about 20 minutes longer. Cut between each rib to separate. Mix mustard and water until smooth; serve with pork.

Meatball Appetizers

30 appetizer meatballs

1   pound ground beef
1   medium onion, chopped (about 1/2 cup)
1/3   cup dry bread crumbs
1/4   cup milk
1   egg
1   teaspoon salt
1/8   teaspoon pepper

Have ready at serving time:

1   cup chili sauce
1/2   cup cold water
1/3   cup currant or grape jelly
1   teaspoon dry mustard

Mix ground beef, onion, crumbs, milk, egg, salt and pepper. Shape mixture into thirty 1-inch balls. Place in ungreased 13 × 9 × 2-inch baking pan. Cook uncovered in 400° oven until done, about 15 minutes. (To serve immediately, continue as directed in TO SERVE except — decrease simmering time to 15 minutes.) Place meatballs on ungreased cookie sheet; freeze uncovered until firm, about 20 minutes. (This partial freezing prevents meatballs from freezing together solidly.) Place partially frozen meatballs in heavy plastic bag or freezer container. Seal, label and freeze no longer than 3 months.

TO SERVE: About 25 minutes before serving, mix chili sauce, water, jelly and mustard in 2-quart saucepan. Add meatballs. Heat to boiling, stirring occasionally; reduce heat. Cover and simmer until meatballs are hot, about 20 minutes. Serve in chafing dish with wooden or plastic picks.

ITALIAN MEATBALLS: Substitute 1 jar (12 ounces) spaghetti sauce for the currant sauce. Sprinkle meatballs with grated Parmesan cheese and snipped parsley if desired.

MEXICAN MEATBALLS: Substitute 1 jar (12 ounces) salsa for the currant sauce. Sprinkle meatballs with thinly sliced green onions (with tops) if desired.

SWEDISH MEATBALLS: Substitute 1 can (10¾ ounces) condensed cream of chicken soup, ¼ cup milk and ½ teaspoon ground nutmeg for the currant sauce. Sprinkle meatballs with dried dill weed if desired.

SWEET-AND-SOUR MEATBALLS: Substitute 1 jar (9½ ounces) sweet-and-sour sauce for the currant sauce.

Glazed Chicken Wings

About 24 appetizers

2   pounds chicken wings (about 12)
1/4   cup honey
2   tablespoons soy sauce
2   tablespoons vegetable oil
2   tablespoons catsup
1   tablespoon lemon juice
1   tablespoon cornstarch
1/2   teaspoon garlic powder

Cut each chicken wing at joints to make 3 pieces; discard tips.

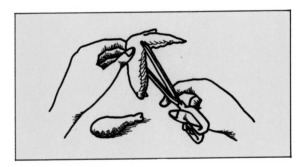

Mix remaining ingredients; pour over chicken. Cover and refrigerate at least 1 hour.

Remove chicken; reserve marinade. Place chicken on rack in foil-lined broiler pan. Cook uncovered in 375° oven, brushing occasionally with reserved marinade, 30 minutes. Turn chicken; cook, brushing occasionally with marinade, until done, about 30 minutes longer. (Can be served immediately.) Refrigerate until cool. Wrap, label and freeze no longer than 3 weeks.

TO SERVE: About 25 minutes before serving, remove Glazed Chicken Wings from freezer and unwrap. Heat on ungreased cookie sheet, in single layer, in 375° oven until hot, about 20 minutes.

Hot Spiced Wine

10 servings - about ³⁄₄ cup each

2	cups pineapple juice
1	cup water
1	cup packed brown sugar
	Peel of 2 oranges, cut into ¹⁄₄-inch strips
¹⁄₂	cup orange juice
6	whole cloves
4	- inch cinnamon stick
3	whole allspice
¹⁄₂	teaspoon salt
1	bottle (⁴⁄₅ quart) dry red wine

Heat pineapple juice, water, brown sugar, orange peel, orange juice, cloves, cinnamon stick, allspice and salt to boiling in 4-quart Dutch oven, stirring occasionally; reduce heat. Simmer uncovered 15 minutes. Remove spices and orange peel; stir in wine. Heat just until hot (do not boil). Serve in mugs or heat-proof glasses garnished with orange slice and cinnamon stick if desired.

NOTE: Hot Spiced Wine can be covered and refrigerated no longer than 1 week. Just before serving, heat just until hot (do not boil).

Spiced Coffee

8 servings - about ²⁄₃ cup each

6	cups water
¹⁄₂	cup packed brown sugar
¹⁄₃	cup freeze-dried instant coffee
1	tablespoon ground cinnamon
2	teaspoons cocoa
¹⁄₂	teaspoon ground cloves
¹⁄₂	teaspoon vanilla

Heat all ingredients except vanilla to boiling; reduce heat. Simmer uncovered 10 minutes. Stir in vanilla.

BRANDIED SPICED COFFEE: Stir in ¹⁄₄ cup brandy with the vanilla. Top each serving with sweetened whipped cream. Sprinkle with ground cinnamon if desired.

Hot Spiced Wine

Ice Cream Beverage

4 to 6 servings - about ½ cup each

Let 1 quart vanilla ice cream stand at room temperature until slightly softened. Place ice cream in blender or mixer bowl with any of the following. Beat on high speed until blended or smooth. Serve immediately with cocktail straw and dessert spoon.

ALMOND: ¼ cup almond-flavored liqueur and ¼ cup white crème de cocoa.

COFFEE: ¼ cup coffee-flavored liqueur and ¼ cup brandy.

FRUIT: 1 package (10 ounces) frozen strawberries, raspberries or peaches, thawed, and 1 tablespoon lemon juice

MOCHA: ½ cup chilled strong coffee and ¼ cup chocolate-flavored syrup.

Tomato Refresher

6 servings - about 1 cup each

1   can (46 ounces) tomato juice
1   can (12 ounces) beer
¼   teaspoon red pepper sauce
½   teaspoon celery salt

Mix all ingredients. Serve over ice. Garnish each serving with celery stick if desired.

Cranberry Cooler

6 servings - about ¾ cup each

1½   cups cranberry juice
      Ice
3   cups dry white wine
6   orange slices

Pour ¼ cup cranberry juice over ice in each of 6 glasses; stir in ½ cup wine. Garnish with orange slice.

Banana Daiquiris

6 servings - about ½ cup each

3   bananas, cut into pieces
¾   cup light rum
¼   cup lime juice
1   tablespoon sugar
12   ice cubes, crushed

Place all ingredients in blender container. Cover and blend on high speed until foamy, about 25 seconds. Serve immediately.

STRAWBERRY DAIQUIRIS: Substitute 1 pint strawberries for the bananas.

EASY COFFEE FIX-UPS

CALIFORNIA COFFEE: For each serving, place 2 tablespoons brandy in a mug. Fill ⅔ full with hot strong coffee. Top with a scoop of chocolate ice cream.

DESSERT COFFEE: For each serving, place 1 to 2 tablespoons chocolate ready-to-spread frosting in coffee cup. Fill with hot coffee; stir until blended. Top with a dollop of whipped cream.

MOCHA ESPRESSO: For each serving, stir 1 tablespoon instant cocoa mix and 2 teaspoons instant espresso coffee into 1 cup hot milk. Sprinkle with ground cinnamon.

TROPICAL COFFEE: For each serving, place 1 tablespoon coconut syrup in a mug; fill with hot strong coffee and stir. Top with whipped cream and sprinkle with flaked coconut.

COFFEE FLOAT: For each serving, fill a tall glass ⅔ full with strong iced coffee; top with a scoop of vanilla ice cream.

ICED COFFEE: Pour cold coffee into divided freezer trays; freeze. To serve, pour hot strong coffee over coffee cubes in a tall glass. Serve with sugar and cream if desired.

Hot Buttered Rum

3 cups batter

1   cup butter
1   cup plus 2 tablespoons packed brown sugar
1   cup whipping cream
2   cups powdered sugar
$1/8$ teaspoon ground cloves
$1/8$ teaspoon ground cinnamon
$1/4$ teaspoon ground nutmeg

Have ready at serving time for each serving:

1   ounce rum (2 tablespoons)
$1/2$ cup boiling water
    Ground nutmeg

Beat butter and brown sugar on medium speed until fluffy, about 5 minutes. Beat in cream and powdered sugar alternately on low speed until smooth. Stir in cloves, cinnamon and nutmeg. (To serve immediately, continue as directed in TO SERVE.) Spoon into 1-quart freezer container. Cover, label and freeze no longer than 3 months.

TO SERVE: For each serving, place rum and 2 tablespoons Hot Buttered Rum in mug. Stir in boiling water; sprinkle with nutmeg.

Frozen Daiquiri

4 to 6 servings - $1/2$ to $3/4$ cup each

1   cup light rum
1   can (6 ounces) frozen limeade concentrate
2   cans water

Mix rum, limeade concentrate and water. Pour rum mixture into refrigerator tray and freeze until slushy, at least 3 hours but no longer than 1 month.

TO SERVE: For each serving, spoon Frozen Daiquiri into glass. Serve with cocktail straw.

FROZEN PINK DAIQUIRI: Substitute pink lemonade concentrate for the limeade concentrate. Garnish with strawberries if desired.

Spiced Tea Mix

About $5 1/4$ cups mix

1   jar (9 ounces) powdered orange breakfast
    drink mix
1   jar (4 ounces) lemon-flavored iced tea mix
$1 1/2$ cups sugar
2   teaspoons ground cinnamon
2   teaspoons ground cloves
1   teaspoon ground ginger

Have ready at serving time for each serving:

1   cup boiling water, cranberry juice or dry red
    or white wine

Mix drink mix, tea mix, sugar and spices. Label and store in tightly covered container at room temperature no longer than 6 months.

TO SERVE: For each serving, mix 3 teaspoons Spiced Tea Mix and the boiling liquid in mug until mix is dissolved. Garnish each with a twist of lemon or orange peel and a cinnamon stick if desired.

Cocoa Mix

About $4 1/2$ cups mix

$2 2/3$ cups nonfat dry milk
$1 1/2$ cups cocoa
1   cup sugar
$1/4$ teaspoon salt

Have ready at serving time for each serving:

2   tablespoons cold milk or water
1   cup hot milk or water

Mix dry milk, cocoa, sugar and salt. Label and store in tightly covered container at room temperature no longer than 6 months.

TO SERVE: For each serving, mix 2 heaping teaspoons Cocoa Mix and the cold milk in mug until smooth. Stir in hot milk. Top with marshmallows if desired.

Hot Buttered Rum, Spiced Tea Mix, and Cocoa Mix

Glazed Apple Rings

Glazed Apple Rings

4 servings

1/4   cup margarine or butter
4   apples, cored and cut into 1/2-inch rings
1/2   cup dry white wine or apple juice
1   tablespoon lemon juice
1/4   teaspoon ground ginger
1/4   teaspoon ground cinnamon
1/2   cup sugar

Heat margarine in 10-inch skillet over medium heat until melted. Fry several apple rings at a time, turning once, until golden brown. (Add more margarine if necessary.) Return all apple rings to skillet. Mix wine, lemon juice, ginger and cinnamon; pour over apples. Sprinkle with sugar. Cover and cook over medium heat just until apples are tender and glazed, about 5 minutes. Serve warm and, if desired, with whipped topping.

Apricot Cream

4 servings

1   can (17 ounces) apricot halves, drained
1   package (3 3/4 ounces) banana-flavored instant pudding and pie filling
1   cup whipping cream

Place apricots in blender container. Cover and blend on high speed until smooth, about 20 seconds. Add pudding and pie filling (dry) and whipping cream. Cover and blend on high speed, stopping blender frequently to scrape sides, until smooth and thickened, about 30 seconds. Divide among 4 dishes; sprinkle with ground nutmeg if desired.

PEACH CREAM: Substitute 1 can (16 ounces) sliced peaches, drained, for the apricots.

Grapes and Sour Cream

4 servings

3   cups seedless green grapes or 2 cans (16 ounces
        each) seedless green grapes, drained
½   cup dairy sour cream
2   tablespoons granulated sugar
     Brown sugar

Divide grapes among 4 dessert dishes. Mix sour cream and granulated sugar; spoon about 2 tablespoons over each serving. Sprinkle with brown sugar.

MIXED FRUITS AND SOUR CREAM: Substitute assorted fresh fruits (strawberries, blueberries, raspberries, sliced peaches, nectarines, melon balls or sliced bananas) for the grapes.

Mexican Fruit Dessert

6 servings

3   oranges, pared and sectioned
3   bananas, sliced
1   pint strawberries, cut into halves
¼   cup coffee-flavored liqueur
1   cup whipping cream
¼   cup powdered sugar
     Ground cinnamon

Toss oranges, bananas and strawberries with liqueur in 2-quart bowl. Beat whipping cream and powdered sugar in chilled 1-quart bowl until stiff. Spread over fruit; sprinkle with cinnamon. Serve immediately.

Double Orange Dessert

4 servings

2   tablespoons sugar
½   teaspoon ground cinnamon
4   large oranges, pared and sectioned
1   pint orange, lemon or lime sherbet

Mix sugar and cinnamon; toss with oranges. Divide oranges among 4 dishes; top with sherbet. Sprinkle with coconut if desired.

Sautéed Pineapple

8 servings

½   cup margarine or butter
1   medium pineapple,* cut into 1-inch pieces
⅓   cup sugar
2   tablespoons orange-flavored liqueur
1   teaspoon grated orange peel
2   tablespoons brandy
     Vanilla ice cream

Heat margarine in 10-inch skillet over medium heat until melted. Stir in pineapple. Cook, stirring constantly, 1 minute. Stir in sugar, liqueur and orange peel. Cook, stirring constantly, 1 minute. Heat brandy in saucepan until warm; ignite and pour over pineapple. Serve over ice cream.

*2 cans (13¼ ounces each) pineapple chunks in juice, drained, can be substituted for the fresh pineapple.

Toasted Cake Toppers

Cut pound cake into ½-inch slices or a loaf angel food cake into 1-inch slices. Set oven control to broil and/or 550°. Broil slices with tops 2 to 3 inches from heat until golden brown, about 40 seconds on each side. Top each slice with one of the following:

Cantaloupe balls or bite-size pieces cantaloupe and lemon sherbet
Sliced banana and hot fudge sauce
Canned peach slices, drained, and frozen raspberries (thawed)
Coffee or chocolate ice cream and coffee-flavored liqueur
Applesauce and maple-nut ice cream
Chocolate ice cream and caramel sauce, sprinkled with salted peanuts or chopped pecans.

EASY FRESH FRUIT DESSERTS

BANANA BOATS: Cut V-shaped wedge lengthwise in each banana. Fill groove with miniature marshmallows and chocolate chips. Wrap each banana in aluminum foil; heat in 450° oven until warm, about 10 minutes.

GRAPEFRUIT GRENADINE: Remove seeds from chilled grapefruit halves. Cut around edges and sections to loosen. Sprinkle each half with 1 to 2 teaspoons grenadine syrup.

MELON AND BERRIES: For each serving, place a scoop of orange sherbet in the center of cantaloupe or Persian melon wedge. Top with blueberries, blackberries or raspberries.

STRAWBERRY FONDUE: Serve strawberries with individual bowls of dairy sour cream and brown sugar. Dip berries into sour cream and then into sugar.

Gingered Pineapple

4 servings

1   pineapple (with green leaves)
1/4   cup dark rum
1   teaspoon ground ginger

Have ready at serving time:

1/2   cup flaked or shredded coconut

Cut pineapple lengthwise into halves through green top; cut each half into halves. Cut core from each quarter and cut along curved edges with grapefruit knife. Cut fruit crosswise into 3/4-inch slices; then cut lengthwise down center of slices. Mix rum and ginger; spoon over pineapple. Cover and refrigerate at least 4 hours but no longer than 24 hours.

TO SERVE: About 15 minutes before serving, cook coconut in 8 × 8 × 2-inch baking pan in 350° oven, stirring occasionally, until golden brown, 8 to 10 minutes. Sprinkle over pineapple quarters. Garnish with strawberries and mint leaves if desired.

Strawberry Cream

6 servings

1   cup boiling water
1   package (3 ounces) strawberry-flavored gelatin
4   to 6 ice cubes
1   cup dairy sour cream
1   can (21 ounces) strawberry pie filling

Pour boiling water over gelatin in 2-quart bowl; stir until gelatin is dissolved. Add ice cubes; stir until gelatin begins to thicken. Remove any unmelted ice. Beat in sour cream with hand beater until smooth. Stir in pie filling. Divide mixture among 6 molds or dessert dishes. Refrigerate at least 4 hours but no longer than 24 hours. Top with whipped cream if desired.

Berry-Almond Dessert

8 servings

2   envelopes (1 tablespoon each) unflavored gelatin
2/3   cup cold water
1   can (14 ounces) sweetened condensed milk
2   cups water
1/4   cup almond-flavored liqueur or 1 tablespoon almond extract
1   quart strawberries,* sliced
1/2   cup sugar

Sprinkle gelatin on 2/3 cup cold water in 2-quart saucepan to soften; heat over low heat, stirring constantly, until gelatin is dissolved. Stir in milk, 2 cups water and the liqueur. Pour into 9 × 9 × 2-inch baking pan. Refrigerate until firm, at least 4 hours but no longer than 24 hours. Mix strawberries and sugar; cover and refrigerate no longer than 24 hours. Cut dessert into 1-inch squares; divide among 8 dessert dishes. Top with strawberries.

*1 package (10 ounces) frozen sliced strawberries, thawed, can be substituted for the strawberries and sugar.

Crème Brûlée

6 servings

3   egg yolks
2   tablespoons granulated sugar
1½ cups whipping cream

Have ready at serving time:

2   cups blueberries, raspberries or sliced
       strawberries
3   nectarines or peaches, thinly sliced
⅓   cup packed brown sugar

Beat egg yolks until thick and lemon colored, about 5 minutes. Gradually beat in granulated sugar. Heat whipping cream in 1½-quart saucepan over medium heat just until hot. Stir at least half of the hot cream gradually into egg yolks. Blend into hot cream in saucepan. Cook, stirring constantly, until mixture thickens, about 5 minutes (do not boil). Pour into 9-inch pie plate. Refrigerate at least 2 hours but no longer than 24 hours.

TO SERVE: About 10 minutes before serving, set oven control to broil and/or 550°. Mix blueberries and nectarines; divide among 6 dessert dishes. Sprinkle brown sugar over Crème Brûlée. Broil with top about 5 inches from heat until sugar melts and forms a glaze, about 3 minutes. Spoon over fruit.

Berries Chantilly

6 servings

2   cups sliced strawberries
1½ cups blueberries
3   tablespoons dry white wine
1   teaspoon grated lime or orange peel
¾   cup whipping cream
2   tablespoons powdered sugar

Mix strawberries, blueberries, wine and lime peel. Divide among 6 dessert dishes. Beat whipping cream and powdered sugar in chilled 1-quart bowl until stiff; spread over berries. Cover and refrigerate at least 8 hours but no longer than 24 hours. Top each with whole strawberry if desired.

Plums in Wine Sauce

6 servings

½   cup water
½   cup sweet red wine
¼   cup sugar
1   tablespoon lemon juice
3 - inch cinnamon stick
6   whole cloves
6   red plums, cut into fourths
6   purple plums, cut into fourths

Heat water, wine, sugar, lemon juice, cinnamon stick and cloves to boiling in 2-quart saucepan. Stir in plums. Heat to boiling. Simmer uncovered just until plums are tender, about 5 minutes. Remove plums with slotted spoon and reserve. Heat wine mixture to boiling; boil uncovered until reduced to ½ cup, about 4 minutes. Remove spices; pour sauce over plums. (Can be served immediately.) Cover and refrigerate, stirring occasionally, at least 3 hours but no longer than 24 hours.

TO SERVE: About 30 minutes before serving, remove plums from refrigerator; let stand at room temperature. Divide among 6 dessert dishes. Top each with sweetened whipped cream or dairy sour cream if desired.

Chocolate Mallow

4 servings

16   large marshmallows or 1½ cups miniature
       marshmallows
⅓   cup water
¼   cup cocoa
½   cup whipping cream

Heat marshmallows, water and cocoa over medium heat, stirring occasionally, until marshmallows are melted. Refrigerate until mixture mounds slightly when dropped from a spoon.

Beat whipping cream in chilled 1-quart bowl until stiff. Fold marshmallow mixture into whipped cream. Spoon into 4 dessert dishes. Cover and refrigerate until firm, at least 3 hours but no longer than 24 hours.

Granola

About 7 cups granola

3 cups oats
1 cup sunflower nuts
1 cup flaked or shredded coconut
1 cup coarsely chopped cashews or
    blanched almonds
1/2 cup packed brown sugar
1/2 cup honey
1/2 cup vegetable oil
1 tablespoon vanilla
3/4 teaspoon ground allspice
1/2 teaspoon salt

Mix oats, sunflower nuts, coconut and cashews in 4-quart bowl. Mix remaining ingredients; toss with oat mixture until evenly coated. Spread in 2 ungreased 15 1/2 × 10 1/2 × 1-inch jelly roll pans. Cook uncovered in 325° oven, stirring frequently, until golden brown, about 30 minutes; cool. Store in tightly covered container in refrigerator no longer than 2 months. Use in Granola Bread (page 106), Peanut Butter Bars (below), Chocolate-Granola Bars (right), Easy Upside-Down Cake (below right), Quick Apricot Dessert (page 143), Peach Delight (page 143) or Ice-Cream Squares (page 143).

FRUITED GRANOLA: Stir 2 cups golden raisins and 1 cup cut-up dried apples, apricots or mixed fruit into oat mixture. 10 cups granola.

Peanut Butter Bars

3 dozen bars

1/2 cup light corn syrup
2/3 cup creamy peanut butter
3 cups Granola (above)

Heat corn syrup to boiling in 3-quart saucepan. Boil 1 minute; remove from heat. Stir in peanut butter until smooth. Stir in Granola. Pat mixture in buttered 9 × 9 × 2-inch baking pan with dampened spatula. Let stand 1 hour. Cut into bars, about 2 × 1 inch.

Chocolate-Granola Bars

3 dozen bars

1/3 cup margarine or butter
4 cups Granola (left)
1 package (6 ounces) semisweet chocolate chips
1 can (14 ounces) sweetened condensed milk

Heat margarine in 13 × 9 × 2-inch baking pan in 325° oven until melted. Rotate pan until margarine covers bottom. Sprinkle 3 cups of the Granola over margarine. Bake 15 minutes; sprinkle with chocolate chips and remaining Granola. Pour milk over top. Bake until light brown, about 20 minutes. While warm, run knife around edges to loosen sides; cool. Cut into bars, about 2 × 1 1/2 inches.

Easy Upside-Down Cake

9 servings

1/2 cup margarine or butter
1 can (8 1/4 ounces) sliced pineapple, drained
4 maraschino cherries
1 1/2 cups Granola (above left)
1 package (13.5 ounces) banana walnut snack cake mix

Heat margarine in 8 × 8 × 2-inch baking pan in 375° oven until melted. Arrange pineapple in pan; place cherry in center of each slice. Sprinkle Granola over pineapple. Prepare cake mix as directed on package except — mix in bowl. Pour over fruit in pan. Bake until cake pulls away from sides of pan and springs back when touched lightly in center, 30 to 35 minutes. Invert onto heatproof plate. Let pan remain a few minutes. Serve warm and, if desired, with whipped cream.

Quick Apricot Dessert

6 servings

1   can (21 ounces) apricot pie filling
1   tablespoon lemon juice
1   cup Granola (page 142)
1/3   cup all-purpose flour
2   tablespoons margarine or butter, melted

Mix pie filling and lemon juice in ungreased 8 × 8 × 2-inch baking pan; spread evenly. Mix remaining ingredients; sprinkle over filling. Cook uncovered in 375° oven until filling is bubbly and topping is golden brown, 20 to 25 minutes. Serve warm and, if desired, with ice cream or cream.

QUICK APPLE DESSERT: Substitute apple pie filling for the apricot pie filling.

QUICK BLUEBERRY DESSERT: Substitute blueberry pie filling for the apricot pie filling.

QUICK CHERRY DESSERT: Substitute cherry pie filling for the apricot pie filling.

Peach Delight

5 or 6 servings

1   can (29 ounces) peach halves, drained
2   tablespoons packed brown sugar
2/3   cup Granola (page 142)
1/4   cup orange marmalade
1/4   cup margarine or butter, melted

Place peach halves, cut sides up, in ungreased 8 × 8 × 2-inch baking pan; sprinkle with brown sugar. Set oven control to broil and/or 550°. Broil peaches with tops about 5 inches from heat until light brown, 2 to 3 minutes.

Mix remaining ingredients; spoon onto peaches. Broil until topping is bubbly and brown, about 1 minute longer. Serve with ice cream if desired.

Ice-Cream Squares

9 servings

4   cups Granola (page 142)
1/4   cup caramel or chocolate ice-cream topping
1   quart vanilla ice cream

Sprinkle 2 cups of the Granola in ungreased 9 × 9 × 2-inch baking pan; drizzle with ice-cream topping. Cut ice cream into about 1-inch slices; place on Granola in pan. Let stand until slightly softened; spread evenly. Sprinkle with remaining Granola. Cover and freeze until firm, about 6 hours. Serve with additional topping if desired.

Ice-Cream Squares

EASY DO-AHEAD DESSERTS

NESSELRODE ICE CREAM: Stir ¼ cup Nesselrode into 1 quart vanilla ice cream, slightly softened. Spoon ice cream mixture into 2 freezer trays and freeze until firm.

GINGERED LEMON SHERBET: Stir ¼ cup finely chopped crystallized ginger into 1 pint lemon sherbet, slightly softened. Freeze until firm, at least 1 hour.

PUMPKIN FROST: Fold 1 can (18 ounces) pumpkin pie mix into 1 quart vanilla ice cream, slightly softened. Divide among 12 paper-lined muffin cups. Cover and freeze until firm, at least 3 hours. To serve, top each with whipped topping and pecan half.

CHOCOLATE ANGEL TORTE: Cut angel food cake loaf horizontally into 3 layers. Beat 1½ cups whipping cream, ¾ cup powdered sugar and ⅓ cup cocoa until stiff. Fill layers and frost sides and top of loaf with cocoa mixture. Sprinkle with chopped nuts. Refrigerate at least 8 hours. 6 to 8 servings.

Basic Cookie Mix

16 cups mix

8   cups all-purpose flour
2½ cups granulated sugar
2½ cups packed brown sugar
2   tablespoons baking powder
1   tablespoon salt
2   teaspoons baking soda
3   cups shortening

Mix flour, sugars, baking powder, salt and baking soda in 6-quart bowl. Cut in shortening with pastry blender just until mixture resembles small peas. Store in airtight container at room temperature no longer than 10 weeks. Use Basic Cookie Mix in Walnut-Orange Bars (above right), Fudgy Brownies (below right), Spicy Pumpkin Bars (page 145), Chocolate Chip Squares (page 145), Cherry-Almond Drops (page 146), Gingersnaps (page 146), Sesame Wafers (page 147), or Chocolate-Brickle Drops (page 147).

Walnut-Orange Bars

3 dozen bars

3   cups Basic Cookie Mix (below left)
3   eggs
½   cup orange marmalade
1   teaspoon vanilla
¼   teaspoon salt
1½   cups finely chopped walnuts
¾   cup packed brown sugar
¼   cup all-purpose flour
½   teaspoon baking powder
     Chocolate Glaze (below)

Heat oven to 375°. Mix cookie mix and 1 egg. Press in ungreased 13 × 9 × 2-inch baking pan. Bake until golden brown, about 10 minutes. Spread with marmalade. Mix remaining eggs, the vanilla, salt, walnuts, brown sugar, flour and baking powder. Spread over marmalade. Bake 25 minutes; cool. Spread with Chocolate Glaze. Cut into bars, about 3 × 1 inch.

Chocolate Glaze

2   squares (1 ounce each) unsweetened chocolate
3   tablespoons margarine or butter
1   tablespoon corn syrup
1   cup powdered sugar
¾   teaspoon vanilla
2   tablespoons hot water

Heat chocolate, margarine and corn syrup until melted; remove from heat. Stir in sugar and vanilla. Beat in water, 1 teaspoon at a time, until glaze is of desired consistency.

Fudgy Brownies

4 dozen squares

¾   cup chocolate-flavored syrup
1   egg
1   teaspoon vanilla
3½   cups Basic Cookie Mix (left)
¾   cup chopped nuts

Heat oven to 350°. Mix syrup, egg, vanilla, mix and nuts. Spread in greased 13 × 9 × 2-inch baking pan. Bake 28 to 32 minutes (do not overbake). Cool; cut into 1½-inch squares.

Spicy Pumpkin Bars

70 bars

1 *can (16 ounces) pumpkin*
½ *cup vegetable oil*
4 *eggs, beaten*
3½ *cups Basic Cookie Mix (page 144)*
1 *teaspoon ground allspice*
1 *cup chopped nuts*
  Cream Cheese Glaze (below)

Heat oven to 350°. Beat pumpkin, oil and eggs on medium speed 1 minute. Stir in mix, allspice and nuts. Pour into greased 15½ × 10½ × 1-inch jelly roll pan. Bake until wooden pick inserted in center comes out clean, 25 to 30 minutes; cool. Spread with Cream Cheese Glaze. Cut into bars, 2 × 1 inch. Store glazed bars in refrigerator.

Cream Cheese Glaze

1 *package (3 ounces) cream cheese, softened*
3 *tablespoons milk*
1 *teaspoon vanilla*
½ *teaspoon ground cinnamon*
2 *cups powdered sugar*

Beat cream cheese, milk, vanilla and cinnamon until creamy. Stir in powdered sugar until glaze is smooth and of desired consistency.

Chocolate Chip Squares

25 squares

3 *cups Basic Cookie Mix (page 144)*
1 *egg*
2 *tablespoons water*
1 *teaspoon vanilla*
1 *package (6 ounces) semisweet chocolate chips*
½ *cup chopped walnuts*

Heat oven to 375°. Mix cookie mix, egg, water and vanilla. Stir in chocolate chips and walnuts. Spread in ungreased 9 × 9 × 2-inch baking pan. Bake until wooden pick inserted in center comes out clean, about 20 minutes; cool. Cut into about 1¾-inch squares.

Walnut-Orange Bars, Spicy Pumpkin Bars, and Chocolate Chip Squares

Cherry-Almond Drops

About 4 dozen cookies

3   cups Basic Cookie Mix (page 144)
1   egg
1   teaspoon almond extract
²/₃ cup chopped maraschino cherries
¹/₂ cup chopped almonds

Heat oven to 375°. Mix cookie mix, egg and almond extract. Stir in cherries and almonds. Drop dough by rounded teaspoonfuls about 2 inches apart onto ungreased cookie sheet. Bake until light golden brown, 8 to 10 minutes. Cool 1 minute before removing from cookie sheet.

DATE-ALMOND DROPS: Substitute vanilla for almond extract and cut-up dates for cherries.

Gingersnaps

About 4 dozen cookies

3   cups Basic Cookie Mix (page 144)
¹/₄ cup dark molasses
1   egg
2   teaspoons ground ginger
1   teaspoon ground allspice
    Sugar

Mix cookie mix, molasses, egg, ginger and allspice. Cover and refrigerate at least 1 hour.

Heat oven to 375°. Shape dough by rounded teaspoonfuls into balls; dip tops in sugar. Place balls, sugared sides up, about 3 inches apart on lightly greased cookie sheet. Bake until edges are set, 10 to 12 minutes (centers will be soft). Immediately remove from cookie sheet.

Cherry-Almond Drops, Gingersnaps, Sesame Wafers, and Chocolate-Brickle Drops

Sesame Wafers

About 3 dozen cookies

⅓   cup sesame seed
3   cups Basic Cookie Mix (page 144)
1   egg
2   tablespoons water
1   teaspoon vanilla

Heat sesame seed over medium heat, stirring frequently, until light brown; cool.

Heat oven to 375°. Mix sesame seed and the remaining ingredients. Drop dough by rounded teaspoonfuls about 2 inches apart onto lightly greased cookie sheet; flatten with greased bottom of glass dipped in sugar. Bake until golden brown, 8 to 10 minutes. Cool 1 minute before removing from cookie sheet.

Chocolate-Brickle Drops

About 5 dozen cookies

3   cups Basic Cookie Mix (page 144)
½   cup chocolate-flavored syrup
1   egg
1   teaspoon vanilla
1   cup quick-cooking oats
¾   cup brickle chips

Heat oven to 350°. Mix cookie mix, syrup, egg and vanilla. Stir in oats and brickle chips. Drop dough by rounded teaspoonfuls about 1 inch apart onto ungreased cookie sheet. Bake until almost no indentation remains when touched, 10 to 12 minutes. Immediately remove from cookie sheet.

Special Helps & Information

Special Dinner For the Family

PLAN-AHEAD DINNER

Savory Beef Short Ribs (page 15)

Poppy Seed Noodles

Whole Green Beans

Carrot Salad (page 87)

Ice Cream Squares (page 143)

SAVED BY THE FREEZER

Beef and Corn Dinners (page 22)

Mashed Potatoes

Freezer Cabbage Salad (page 88)

Toasted Breadsticks (page 102)

Hot Fudge Sundaes

WEEKEND BRUNCH

Eggs-stuffing Casserole (page 72)

Bacon or Sausage

Broccoli Spears

Fruit and Spinach Salad (page 84)

Spiced Coffee (page 134)

EASY DINNER FOR FOUR

Broiled Pork Chops

Parslied Rice

Southern Corn (page 92)

Freezer Cucumber Salad (page 88)

Chocolate Mallow (page 141)

WHEN THE KIDS COOK

Spaghetti With Franks (page 32)

Buttered Peas

Lettuce Wedge with French Dressing

Golden Breadsticks (page 102)

Double Orange Dessert (page 139)

HELPER IN THE KITCHEN

Mexican Bean Patties (page 74)

Steamed Rice

Sautéed Artichoke Hearts (page 91)

California Salads (page 84)

Apricot Cream (page 138)

DINNER FOR GUESTS

Frozen Daiquiri (page 137)

Brie with Almonds (page 130)

Fruited Pot Roast (page 11)

Potato Puffs (page 94)

Broccoli Spears with Lemon

Lettuce and Mushroom Salad (page 81)

Berry-Almond Dessert (page 140)

OFF-THE-SHELF DINNER

Chicken and Noodles (page 44)

Cranberry Sauce

Toasted Breadsticks (page 102)

Sliced Bananas

Cocoa (page 137)

MENU PLANNING

Plan menus for a week at a time, viewing each day as a whole to maintain a nutritional balance. Begin with meat or other protein food, then vegetable and salad, add potatoes, pasta or rice and bread. Use the following Daily Food Guide to select the necessary number of servings from each group.

Fruits and Vegetables: 4 basic servings.
A serving is ½ cup of most vegetables, 1 cup raw salad greens, 1 potato and 1 orange or ½ grapefruit daily; 1 yellow or dark green vegetable every other day.

Breads and Cereals: 4 basic servings.
A serving is 1 slice bread, ½ to ¾ cup cooked cereal, pasta, rice, grits or cornmeal or 1 cup ready-to-eat cereal. Choose whole grain, enriched, restored or fortified products.

Milk and Cheese: 2 servings for adults; 3 for children; 4 for teenagers.
A serving is 1 cup milk, two 1-inch cubes or thin slices cheese, 1½ cups cottage cheese or cream soup, 1½ cups ice cream.

Meat, Poultry and Fish: 2 basic servings.
A serving is 2 to 3 ounces cooked lean meat, poultry or fish; 2 eggs; 1 cup cooked dried beans or peas, 4 tablespoons peanut butter or other nut butters; 1 to 1½ cups nuts; ½ cup seeds.

Fats, Sweets and Alcohol: Servings vary according to caloric needs.
Servings include margarine or butter, mayonnaise or salad dressings, jams, syrup, sugared beverages, candy, wine, beer and liquor.

The best meals look as attractive as they are delicious and nutritious. When planning foods to eat together, think in terms of contrast. Serve hot foods with cold; brightly colored foods with pale foods; and large with small pieces of varying shapes. There should also be a variety of textures varying from crisp to firm to soft whenever possible. Flavors should contrast — spicy with bland, and salty with sweet, for maximum satisfaction.

Concentrate on simple desserts — fruit and cheese, ice cream or sherbet, fresh fruit and cookies. Introduce variety into breakfast rather than serving cereal and eggs day after day. Serve a peanut butter and jelly or grilled cheese sandwich some morning with a glass of milk and fresh fruit. Try to minimize the salt and sugar of packaged snacks in favor of fresh fruits and raw vegetables, yogurt, nutritious cereal bars or cookies and milk or fruit juices. In all, let variety be your guide when selecting food.

AFTER MENUS COMES SHOPPING

Check all the recipes you will be using after planning your week's menus and snacks. Be sure all the staples are on hand and make a list of all other ingredients you will need. The following tips will make your grocery shopping timesaving and economical.

Make copies of a permanent shopping list so you can simply check off items most often needed. Organize the categories in the same order as the supermarket to save time shopping. Keep it handy to jot down staple items as they are needed.

Note advertised specials and incorporate them into your menus. But stay flexible; you may find unadvertised bargains as well.

Shop once a week for the majority of the groceries. Sometimes, due to lack of storage space or the availability of fresh ingredients, all items cannot be purchased at one time.

Shop at one location when possible, to save gas, energy and time. A special trip for a few pennies' price advantage is not economical unless you are making a special purchase to stock your freezer.

Shop when the stores are least crowded and produce is fresh, if you can.

Divide the shopping list between you, if you are shopping with a family member, to accomplish the task in half the time.

KEEP AN ORGANIZED KITCHEN

Store all equipment and utensils close to where they will be used. Store seldom-used items out of the way.

Arrange kitchen cabinets so all items are easy to see and reach. Group similar food and equipment items and store them as near as possible to the place where they will be used.

Use drawer dividers, special racks or holders to keep kitchen utensils organized.

Purchase extras of small utensils, such as measuring cups, measuring spoons and rubber scrapers, to make meal preparation easier. This will eliminate having to wash them between measuring different ingredients.

Clean up as you work during meal preparation to avoid a messy work area and to save time cleaning up after the meal.

Replace covers and lids on containers as soon as they are used to prevent accidental spills which take time to clean up.

Wipe up spills and spatters as soon as they happen because it takes more time to wipe up dried-on spills than fresh ones. Keep a dampened cloth or paper towel handy.

Wash or soak pans and bowls as soon as they are used to prevent food from drying on, which takes additional time to remove later.

EASY TIMESAVING TIPS

Use ingenuity in teaming up foods that can cook together in the same pan or at the same oven temperature. Combine 2 frozen vegetables; if they cook for different lengths of time, begin one and then add the other. Meat loaf from the freezer and baked potatoes can share the same oven.

Avoid too many foods on one menu that require last-minute preparation. It is good to combine do-ahead recipes with quick and easy recipes to balance time. This is especially important when you are entertaining.

Keep dried herbs and seasoning on hand to use as timesaving substitutes. Substitute 1 teaspoon dried or ¼ teaspoon ground herbs for 1 tablespoon snipped herbs, 1 teaspoon parsley flakes for 2 teaspoons snipped fresh parsley, ⅛ teaspoon garlic powder or ¼ teaspoon instant minced garlic for 1 clove garlic and 1 teaspoon onion powder or 2 tablespoons minced onion or onion flakes for ½ cup chopped onion.

Use kitchen shears to snip fresh parsley, chives and herbs. Place them in a measuring cup to prevent scattering and to measure all in one step.

To save time shaping meatballs, shape the meat mixture into a rectangle about 1 inch thick. Cut the mixture into 1-inch squares. You can either cook the squares or shape them into balls.

Use freezer-to-oven-to-table casseroles to save time and cleanup.

Change the style of serving meals to meet time limitations. Sometimes it can save time to serve from the kitchen or buffet-style rather than family-style.

When homemade beef or chicken broth is not available and you need it for a recipe, a quick substitute for each cup of broth is to dissolve 1 bouillon cube or 1 teaspoon instant bouillon in 1 cup boiling water.

Plan a "make-your-own-salad" or "make-your-own-sandwich" meal on an evening when there is limited time for cooking. It is an excellent way to use leftover sliced cooked meats, salad greens, cooked vegetables and odds-and-ends of cheese, breads and fruits. Serve with bottled salad dressing or sandwich spreads. Arrange the ingredients on colorful paper plates or bowls to save cleanup time.

MICROWAVE TIPS

Use your microwave whenever you can to save time when preparing recipes. The following tips can become part of recipe preparation.

Melt margarine or butter uncovered on high (100%) in microwaveproof custard cup, measuring cup or casserole. It takes 15 to 30 seconds to melt 1 to 2 tablespoons, 30 to 45 seconds for 3 to 4 tablespoons, 45 to 60 seconds for ⅓ to ½ cup, and 60 to 90 seconds for ⅔ to 1 cup.

Soften margarine or butter uncovered on microwaveproof dish on medium-low (30%) until softened, allowing 15 to 30 seconds for 1 to 3 tablespoons, and 30 to 45 seconds for ¼ to 1 cup.

Heat water to boiling by microwaving 1 cup hot water on high (100%) 2 to 3 minutes.

Cook bacon on microwaveproof plate lined with 2 paper towels and cover with paper towel before microwaving. Microwave on high (100%) allowing ¾ to 2 minutes for 1 to 2 slices, 2¼ to 3 minutes for 3 slices, 3 to 4 minutes for 4 slices, 3¾ to 5 minutes for 5 slices, and 4 to 6 minutes for 6 slices.

Soften brown sugar by covering tightly and microwaving on high (100%), checking every 30 seconds, until soft.

Soften cream cheese by removing foil wrapper from 3-ounce or 8-ounce package. Microwave uncovered in microwaveproof bowl or pie plate on medium (50%) until softened. (Cheese will hold its shape while it softens.) It will take 30 to 45 seconds for 3 ounces and 60 to 90 seconds for 8 ounces.

EQUIPMENT TIMESAVERS

For the person on the go, for whom time and energy-saving have a high priority, today's technologies offer four items in addition to the range, refrigerator and freezer, which significantly reduce the amount of time and energy once spent in routine kitchen tasks.

FOOD PROCESSORS AND BLENDERS

The food processor has been welcomed into the kitchen as the great timesaver it is for chores like chopping, grinding, shredding, slicing and blending foods. By planning the sequence in which you will use it, you can do a variety of tasks from chopping dry ingredients and vegetables, to slicing and shredding vegetables and cheese, to chopping meat, and only wash the bowl once.

The food processor can be used to chop nuts, vegetables, Parmesan cheese, and some fruits. Watch timing; it is very easy to overprocess food during chopping, so check often. Use it to make bread and cracker crumbs and to slice ingredients for stir-frying, salads and cole slaw.

Less expensive than the food processor, the blender is a familiar and much-used appliance in many kitchens. With it, you can chop, mix, liquefy and blend foods and liquids. An optional attachment for most models allows you to crush ice as well. Study the manufacturer's directions for your model. As with your food processor, keep your blender in a convenient place and learn to use it often.

PRESSURE COOKERS

A pressure cooker can be valuable for anyone with limited time who wishes to use the less-tender, economical cuts of meat. The operation of a pressure cooker is simple, but follow the manufacturer's directions exactly.

In a matter of minutes, the pressure cooker can duplicate the results of hours of slow simmering. It can produce flavorful, tender meats and stews in less than an hour. Browning meat before cooking enhances the flavor and appearance. Since tenderness of meats varies, it is best to undercook, then add cooking time if necessary. Do not cook meat from the frozen state in a pressure cooker because the center will not cook sufficiently.

MICROWAVES

The time and energy saved by microwaves over conventional cooking can be substantial, once the techniques and food preparation sequence are learned. Moreover, cleanup chores are substantially reduced and the microwave can be operated by other family members to reheat foods, cook meals and prepare snacks and hot beverages in minutes.

When the directions state to cover loosely, it means to cover the dish with paper towel, napkin or waxed paper, or place lid ajar. Covering loosely helps prevent spattering and contain heat. Covering tightly with lid or plastic wrap (turn one corner back to prevent splitting) speeds heating by keeping the heat in. Stirring helps cook food more rapidly and should be done from outside to center since food heats faster on the outside. Some directions recommend that the food stand after microwaving to complete the cooking.

Use non-metal utensils made of paper (except color-printed or recycled paper), glass, plastic or ceramic, which contains no metal or metal trim. Choose lightweight, dishwasher-safe utensils with handles and in stackable shapes.

Read manufacturers' manual for your unit for recommendations on use of aluminum foil or foil-lined cooking containers. In general, avoid metal utensils of any kind.

YOUR REFRIGERATOR AND FREEZER

Think of your refrigerator as a safe-deposit box, offering short-term storage for fresh foods and foods prepared a day or two ahead. They are ready to use, eliminating the time necessary to defrost food from the freezer.

The freezer allows you to cook ahead when you have time, then freeze foods for days when an unpredictable work load or an emergency taxes your time and energy. And because you can buy and freeze foods in season, you can enjoy them at peak quality all year-round. Just make sure that everything that goes into your freezer is in prime condition when you buy it, and freeze it promptly.

RED SPOON RECIPES

The "do-ahead" recipes marked with a red spoon symbol have been developed to help you make the most of your refrigerator and freezer. Each recipe begins with the servings, and for some, the number of meals it provides. Each recipe states recommended storage time, which has been determined in the Betty Crocker Kitchens. It indicates how long the food will remain at optimum quality, although it may still be edible beyond that date.

REFRIGERATOR TIPS

Store meats and poultry in their original wrapping up to 2 days in the coldest part of the refrigerator. For longer storage, loosen the wrapping and rewrap loosely to allow air to reach the surface of the meat. This helps to retard bacteria development.

Store fresh fish up to 2 days in the coldest section of the refrigerator.

Eggs should be refrigerated promptly either in original carton or with large ends up so that the yolks remain suspended in the center. They should be used within 1 week.

Refrigerate milk, cream and whipping cream in their original containers, and dairy sour cream in the coldest part of the refrigerator.

Hard cheese such as Cheddar, Swiss or Parmesan will retain its quality for several months when refrigerated unopened in their original wrappers or wrapped tightly in aluminum foil or plastic wrap.

Store cleaned vegetables in the crisper compartment or in plastic bags.

Let fruit ripen at room temperature; then refrigerate and use as soon as possible.

FREEZING TIPS

Line dish with heavy-duty aluminum foil for efficient use of baking dishes or casseroles, allowing extra foil to wrap finished food in. After cooking the food, bring sides of foil up and wrap food securely and label. Freeze in dish until firm; then remove wrapped food and return it to the freezer, leaving the dish available for other uses. Heat food in original baking dish.

Package food in airtight, moisture- and vapor-proof materials such as heavy-duty foil and plastic wrap, bags or tightly-covered containers recommended for freezer use. Eliminate air from packages and wrap tightly, sealing with tape. Wrap easily crushed foods in foil, seal in rigid containers and wrap again.

Label each package with felt-tip pen or grease pencil. Note name of food or recipe and number of other packages of same food; number of servings, weight or any additional preparation for a specific recipe. Calculate the "use by" date and add it to the label. Finally, list any ingredients to be added at serving time and keep a note of any special heating instructions.

Set your freezer at a temperature of 0°F or lower to preserve foods at their best texture and flavor. Freeze food quickly and only as much at a time as can be placed against a freezing surface. Allow at least 1 inch of space around each so that air can circulate. When food is frozen solid, restack packages to conserve space.

Keep a record nearby of the freezer contents; consult it when planning meals and making shopping lists. Record the date the food is frozen and also the date by which it should be used. When you remove food from the freezer, delete the entry on your record.

Take advantage of specials and unexpected sale prices on meats. To save freezer space, trim excess fat and bone before freezing.

Layer ground beef patties, steaks and chops between double sheets of freezer wrap so they separate easily, or freeze in a single layer on cookie sheets, then transfer to freezer bags.

Foods won't stick together, and you can select the number you need.

Prepackaged meats from the supermarket can be frozen up to 2 weeks in store wrapping. However, for longer freezing, remove meat from store wrapping and wrap in moisture- and vapor-proof paper.

Layer fish steaks and fillets between double thickness of aluminum foil or waxed paper so they are easy to separate. Wrap tightly, label and freeze.

FREEZING MEATS, POULTRY AND FISH	
Type	Time (0°F)
Fresh meats (roasts, chops and steaks)*	6 to 9 months
Ground beef, lamb and veal	3 to 4 months
Ground pork and sausage	2 months
Variety meats (liver, heart, tongue)	3 to 4 months
Cooked meats	2 months
Whole or half ham (unsliced)**	2 months
Bacon (unsliced)	3 months
Fresh chicken and turkey	9 months
Cooked chicken and turkey in broth or gravy	1 month 6 months
Giblets	3 months
Cod, yellow perch, haddock and pollack	9 months
Lake bass, flounder and sole	7 to 8 months
White fish, northern pike and shrimp	4 to 5 months

*Prepackaged meat from the supermarket can be frozen in the store wrap up to 2 weeks. For longer storage, remove store wrap and wrap meat in moisture- and vapor-proof wrapping.

**Cured meats such as ham slices, frankfurters, sliced bacon and luncheon meats lose quality rapidly when frozen.

PLAN-AHEAD TIPS

Remove from freezer any item on the menu that needs to be thawed in the refrigerator the evening before or morning of the meal.

Consult your recipes and assemble ingredients and equipment in the order needed before you begin to prepare a meal.

Start the longest cooking food on the menu first. Put a frozen casserole in the oven and, while it cooks, prepare the rest of the meal.

Combining do-ahead and quick-and-easy recipes for the same meal can be the most efficient way to use limited time wisely.

Plan ahead so you can reuse measuring cups and spoons. Measure dry ingredients before wet to save washing time.

Learn to dovetail steps when preparing meals. While water is boiling for the pasta and vegetable, set the table and prepare a quick salad.

When chopping onions or nuts or shredding cheese, do more than the recipe calls for. Store the "plan overs" in recipe amounts in the freezer or refrigerator so they are ready when you need them.

Keep cleaned, crisp vegetable relishes in the refrigerator for quick, nutritious snacks or for a last minute salad at mealtime.

Keep canned fruits in the refrigerator to be used for a quick salad or dessert.

Have canned meats, vegetables and fruits on hand for quick emergency meals.

Frozen whipped cream dollops in the freezer are quick dessert toppers. Just freeze small mounds of whipped cream on a cookie sheet. When they are firm, move them to a tightly covered freezer container. They thaw in about 30 minutes in the refrigerator.

Have olives, pickles, nuts, marinated vegetables, pickled fruits, assorted crackers, cheese, chips and pretzels on hand to serve as no-work appetizers when unexpected guests stop in.

Cook on weekends or plan a few hours during the week for cooking to keep the freezer and refrigerator stocked for quick meals when time is limited.

Get a head start on another meal by roasting meat along with a pan of oven-fried chicken to reheat or serve cold the next day.

It pays to think ahead! Prepare a hot vegetable to serve with cold meats from the deli, or marinate cooked or canned vegetables to serve with broiled hamburgers or chops.

Use a casserole from the freezer on days when someone is home earlier than you are. He or she can put the casserole in the oven and set the table. When you arrive home, the main dish is almost ready and either you or the other person can prepare a quick salad and dessert.

Plan a time when you are at home, to start a recipe that uses a less tender cut of meat, such as pot roast or beef stew, for dinner the next evening. The meat can simmer while you are doing other things. When the meat is tender, cover and refrigerate the meat and broth. The next evening, just heat the meat and broth to boiling, add remaining ingredients such as vegetables, and continue to cook. You can have homemade beef stew in 30 to 45 minutes.

Write and leave meal preparation schedules and instructions for other members of the family so they can start or prepare the meal when you know you will be home late.

Keep your family's favorite convenience products on hand, such as packaged dinner mixes, potato mixes, canned soups, pudding mixes and cookie mixes. They are convenient for mealtime emergencies when you will be later than planned, and they are easy for other members of the family to prepare.

Have a supply of colorful paper or plastic items such as plates, cups, bowls, napkins and place mats. They save cleanup time and can also add a bright touch to a quick meal. For example, use white china plates with bright-colored paper napkins and matching colored plastic glasses. It takes very little time to do and can make a meal more enjoyable after a busy working day.

Index